Cat Chakras

A complete guide to clearing, cleansing and balancing your cats' core energy centres.

By Julie-Anne Thorne

Naturally Cats

This book is intended to give cat guardians an overview of the chakra system in cats. It does not replace veterinary care or diagnosis.

Energy work is a complementary modality and can be used, if needed, alongside conventional treatment for a cat.

The author and publisher assume no liability in connection with use of the information presented in this book.

Copyright 2023 Julie-Anne Thorne.

No part of this book may be used, reproduced or transmitted in any form, or by any means, including photocopying, scanning, reproduced for the internet or by any information storage means without written permission of the author, except where required by law.

All interior photographs property of Julie-Anne Thorne.

Table of contents

Acknowledgements	7
Foreword	8

Part 1 – How to heal

Introduction	12
Connecting with your cat	15
What is harming our cats today?	16
What is energy?	18
Blockages	24
Medication	26
The holistic approach to healing	27
What is healing?	29
The aura	31
The importance of nature	33
Balancing the aura	35
A breakdown of the aura	36
What is intuition and how can we use it?	37
How to receive information	39
What are chakras?	44
The seven main chakras	50
Mirroring	52
Energy and emotions	55
Healing tools	57
Crystals	60
Remedies	64

Herb gardens   65
Essential oils   67
Colour/sound   70
Mantras   73
Pendulum   74
Food   78
Animal communication   80
Meditation   82
Massage   83
Energy movement in the cat   86
Energy processing and energy release   88
Cat responses to processing energy   88
Cat responses to energy release   90
Human responses to energy movement   93

Part 2 – The Chakra System

Root chakra   99
Sacral chakra   105
Solar plexus chakra   111
Heart chakra   117
Throat chakra   121
Third eye chakra   128
Crown chakra   132
How to manage energy   136
What is grounding?   138
What is protecting?   139
Calm connection   141

4

The cat's energy	143
Setting the scene for a chakra clearing	144
Environment	145
What does the cat need?	146
When is the right time to heal your cat?	147
How to sense an imbalance	148
Sensing energy	151
Removing stagnant energy	156
Reducing and increasing energy	159
Opening, closing and protecting the chakras	160
How to conduct the session	161
Aftercare advice	166
Final words	168
Appendices	171
Recommended reading	171
Mantras for healing	172
Cat chakra quick reference guides	173
Chakras and common conditions	180
Index	183
About Julie-Anne Thorne	188

Acknowledgements

Thank you to my sister.

I wouldn't be where I am today without your constant love, support and belief in me.
I am giving cats a voice with you by my side.

Thank you to Pickle.

You changed my life. I hope you are at peace now, Baby Girl. I miss you. This book came to be because of you. The journey you took me on, the lessons you showed me, the path you guided me down …

YOU. ROCKED. MY. WORLD.

I will always love you.

Thank you to my current cats Leo and Baby Max.

Boys… You keep me on my toes! You show me how to love and continue to teach me, every single day. I am a better human for knowing both of you and feel honoured to be your guardian in this time and space.

Foreword

By Dr Katie Woodley.

"We often stumble upon holistic medicine as a last resort when we – or our pets – get poorly and we're told there's nothing else we can do. My journey to finding holistic medicine as a veterinarian was exactly this experience. Through navigating autoimmune disease with my husband and my pets with cancer, I realised that conventional medicine could only do so much for my family. I became a certified practitioner of Chinese herbal medicine, acupuncture, and food therapy so I could provide better treatment options for my family and my clients.

Meeting Julie-Anne Thorne took my understanding of holistic health to another level. She helped me to see that healing is not just about which supplement or food to choose. It goes much deeper than this; sadly, it's this part that is commonly missed by many pet guardians and even vets. Julie-Anne truly opened my eyes to a new way of healing, to break open and heal on a deeper level through energy by being able to connect with our cat companions.

Hearing Julie-Anne's story with her dear Pickle and how she helped her cat by connecting with her energetically was fascinating for me.

I've had the pleasure of working closely with Julie-Anne for several years through my own cats, as she gave me insights into their chakra health. Her feedback and suggestions made a huge difference to our feline family. We now have coloured blankets around the house that my three black cats love to work with, all thanks to Julie-Anne.

I also refer many of my clients to receive complementary therapy with Julie-Anne so that they can learn how to assess and help their cats obtain true healing and resolution of their conditions at an energetic level.

At times I haven't been sure why one of my cats wasn't feeling their best, but after Julie-Anne connects with them, there is a clear path forward to help them heal their blocked chakras through the tools Julie-Anne provides. Her skill set is incredible and is showcased throughout this book with the many examples of how she heals and supports not only her own cats, but also those of her clients.

The clear, detailed instructions that Julie-Anne provides are a true testament to how easy she is to work with to provide our cats with the transformations that so many pet guardians are looking for but have a hard time finding through veterinary medicine alone.

This book is much needed in the cat health space to provide more tools for cat guardians to explore and understand how to help their cats heal on physical and energetic levels while also providing tools to prevent disease through the chakras.

Every cat guardian should own a copy of this book so that you can learn how to connect and heal your cats on a much deeper level that is truly needed in the stress-filled, emotionally strained world that we live in today.

Healing your cat's chakras is a complementary therapy to other treatment modalities, and Julie-Anne provides a clear and concise guide to support your cat on an energetic level. I am forever grateful for the tools that Julie-Anne has provided me to better serve not only my own patients but also to help my own cats live their best and healthiest lives at a much deeper energetic level."

Dr Katie Woodley, BVSc, cVMA, GDVCHM

The Natural Pet Doctor

www.thenaturalpetdoctor.com

Part 1

How to heal

Introduction

'She found me. I'm saved after months of living on the streets, feeling scared and alone. Broken. Finally, it's time to be with her. Time to help her see, to awaken her. Let the healing begin. It's time to share the story.'
- Pickle

Cats have been in my life for as long as I can remember, from our first kittens, Sam and Missey, when I was six years old, to my current boys, Leo and Baby Max. My grandparents had cats, as did my parents and my aunties. Being around cats felt very safe for me; it brought me comfort. I felt I could be myself around them because they didn't expect me to be a certain way or place too many demands on me. I would naturally gravitate to cats wherever I went, and when I left education, I couldn't wait to get my own.

After university, I found Pickle, and she turned out to be the cat that would change the course of my life.

She looked grumpy due to her fur markings and was incredibly poorly for many years. Pickle guided me to train in several complementary therapies, and she rocked my world. I'll share our story with you throughout this book.

Pickle was overweight and had white stripes around her eyes that made her look like she was constantly frowning. She would rub her gorgeous, fluffy face along the side of mine when I held her for cuddles. Heaven.

Before she was put to sleep in October 2019, she suffered from diabetes, pancreatitis, arthritis, gingivitis, obesity and gunky ears. She was very unwell, and I knew she wouldn't get better through conventional, Western medicine alone.

We had a long journey of vet visits, medications and constantly changing symptoms that frustrated us both. Another symptom, another vet visit, another tablet. It wasn't how I wanted to support her, and she wasn't getting any better. I had a nagging feeling that there must be more I could do to help her. But what?

She guided me to my path of animal healing, self-selection, chakra sensing, Reiki and cat communication. I learnt it all to try to help her get better. I had no idea that our journey would put me on a course that created a way to help other cats too.

Our struggles taught me that I want other cats to heal too, not to suffer the way she did. I need people to know that there are other treatments that can support Western medicine.

In this book, I will share with you an overview of my 15+ years' experience working with cats and complementary treatments. I'll give you the tools and techniques you can use to help your cat, to support its health and well-being, so they don't have to suffer the way Pickle did.

I know my journey with Pickle was for a higher purpose. Part of that purpose is this book in which I'll show you the simple steps you need to take to start your own healing journey.

After reading this book, you will be able to offer your cat additional support through healing. If you follow the guidance I have laid out, you will be able to help your cat to heal, as I did Pickle.

Connecting with your cat

Cats are more than just their physical bodies. They are sentient, sensitive, unique beings that can guide us through life if we let them. Your cat will guide you to implement the teachings in this book; they will show you how to help them heal. You just need to listen.

You have the capacity to connect with your cat to clear, cleanse and balance their 'chakras'. Their what? Well, let me explain. The chakra system is essentially a map that helps to identify imbalances in the physical and emotional bodies. Once you understand it, you will see how simple yet powerful it can be.

Energy is the key that you need to understand and harness before you can use the map of your cat's seven chakras to heal him/her. I will show you how energy can be harnessed and used later in this book. Once you are able to sense and feel the Universal energy, you will be able to direct it to your cat to clear energetic blockages and to balance their core energy centres.

Energy healing is a form of medicine that dates back thousands of years. In fact, there is evidence of the early Egyptians using energy healing and colour therapy to heal their sick, the latter of which I'll talk about later.

What is harming our cats today?

Given the alarming rate at which technology is advancing and developing in the world today, is it any wonder that our feline friends are suffering from stress, anxiety and displaying 'problem behaviours'?

Man has domesticated the cat and now we are asking them to live in our busy, toxic environments. Indeed, our cats are exposed to an untold number of toxins every day in their environment. These include Wi-Fi, listening devices, cleaning products, scented air products, highly processed foods, our emotions, other animals in the home and so much more.

As their guardians, we owe them the capacity to heal, to enable our cats to take time out, just as humans need to do from time to time. They need rest to help recharge and heal their physical, mental, emotional and spiritual states.

This book will help you to understand each of the main seven chakras in cats. You will understand how an imbalanced chakra will present itself in your cats' behaviour and body language, and I'll share with you a range of tools you can use to create balance and wellness in your feline friend.

The tools and techniques in this book can be used by any cat guardian; you don't need specific qualifications to tap into your inner healing power. You may just need a little practice.

Every human has the capacity to channel, direct and work with the universal healing energy. If I can do it, so can you. I'll guide you through each of the chakras in turn, share with you how to feel their energies and to balance them to support the wellness of your cat, enabling it to thrive. You can't get this wrong; if your intention is to heal your cat, the Universal energy will flow through you.

I started my journey by sitting on the sofa with Pickle, desperate to help her, the mantra, 'Help me heal her', running on a loop in my mind as my hand lay on her tummy.

With no training or qualifications other than my Psychology Degree, which definitely didn't cover healing for cats, I helped her. How do I know? Because after our time on the sofa, we checked her blood glucose level (she was diabetic) and she had the lowest reading I had ever seen. My mind was blown, my heart skipped a beat. And our healing journey began.

Now, let's start yours.

What is energy?

Everything is made of energy. Energy is moving particles. It might be easy to understand that humans, animals and nature are made up of energy, as we can see things changing. The seasons, our physical body and wounds healing, for example. Yet even static items, such as a bookcase, are made of energy, moving particles. We just can't see them with the naked eye because the matter is so dense.

A fundamental element of energy is vibration – the movement of particles to and fro.

The other is frequency – the measurement of how often the moving particles vibrate every second.

Energy is measured using frequency, and this is determined by vibration.

I'm not going to delve too deeply into the science of this, but for the purposes of this book, it's important to understand that we can directly impact the vibration and frequency around us. That means we can change and manipulate the moving particles of energy. When we feel the energy by finding its vibration, we can change it. It's like tuning a radio to find a specific signal: when you find the station you want, you can hear the radio show. That's what I will help you do – to find the frequency of your cat's chakras so you can receive the information from them. When you know what state they are in, you can set about using the tools in this book to clear, cleanse and balance them.

As I've said, you don't need to have any specific qualifications to feel energy. Anyone can do it, although it might take a little practice.

Everyone will have felt energy at some point in his/her life. Have you ever walked into a room and thought, 'You could cut the atmosphere with a knife'? That is energy that you are feeling. Or perhaps you've had a 'weird' experience that you can't explain – your hands suddenly getting hot or being near an animal and your feelings change. Energy is all around us; we just need to tune into it.

In traditional healing, energy is referred to as Chi and/or Prana and is considered the vital life force of any being. It runs through us and around us every minute of every day.

Science can prove, beyond doubt, that the body and mind are made of energy, and they can both create and change it. Energy is used by the cells in our body, the functions of the systems that keep the body alive.

The physical body is surrounded by an energy field called the 'aura' (more on this on page 31), which is influenced by internal and external factors.

The physical body is a compressed version of the spiritual body. Therefore, when we start to shift the energy in the spiritual body, the physical body is impacted. Hence when I was sitting with Pickle on the sofa, holding the intention to heal her, it shifted her spiritual body – her energy – which in turn affected her physical body, her blood glucose level.

Energy is influenced by emotions, intention, environment, behaviour and actions. So, if a cat is scratching the sofa and constantly being shouted at by its guardian, it will impact its energy. It is likely to make the cat afraid and confused. After all, it is behaving like a normal cat and won't understand why it is being shouted at. Repetition of this interaction is likely to cause a 'blockage' of energy through trapped emotion as the cat cannot express itself. You will learn more about blockages in the section of that name further on.

On the flip side of this, if a cat has frequent loving interactions with a human, such as a brushing session that it enjoys, it will help to increase the cat's energy by raising its vibration.

Emotions are energy. I like to think of it as E-motion, energy in motion. Emotions affect a cat's energetic vibration. A cat's emotional state is directly linked to its physical health, mental health, vibration and frequency.

You can see from the vibrational scale table the difference in vibration and frequency that the range of emotion has. When a cat is angry or frustrated, it will be in a lower, dense vibration. This inhibits the flow of energy and life force through its body and auric field, which is discussed in more detail in 'The aura' chapter.

VIBRATIONAL SCALE

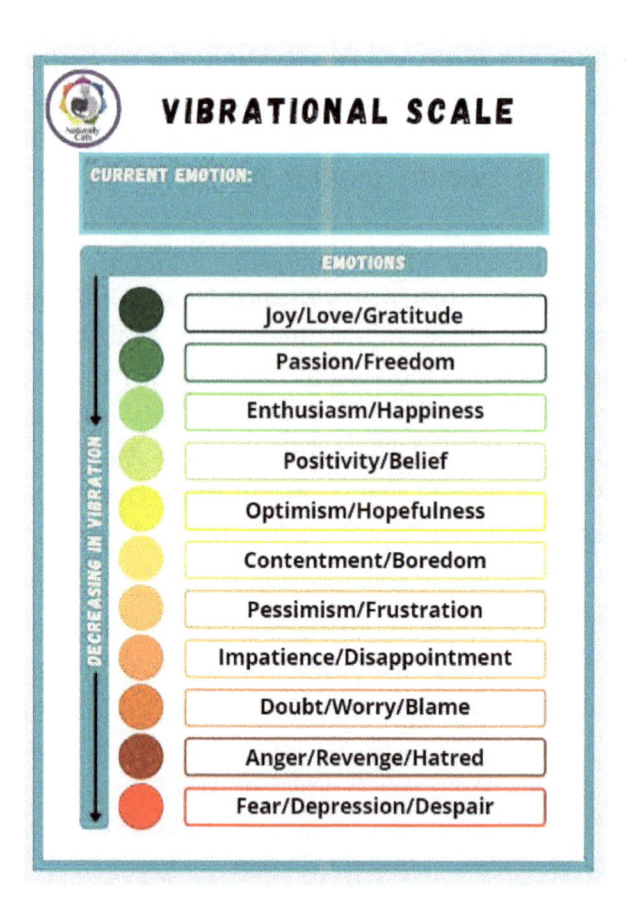

CURRENT EMOTION:

EMOTIONS

DECREASING IN VIBRATION ↓

- Joy/Love/Gratitude
- Passion/Freedom
- Enthusiasm/Happiness
- Positivity/Belief
- Optimism/Hopefulness
- Contentment/Boredom
- Pessimism/Frustration
- Impatience/Disappointment
- Doubt/Worry/Blame
- Anger/Revenge/Hatred
- Fear/Depression/Despair

When a cat is happy, it experiences joy, which is a lighter, higher-vibration emotion that will help its energy to flow more consistently.

A cat's physical body has several forms of energy active at any one time. These are:

- Immune system
- Hormonal system
- Respiratory system
- Cardiovascular system
- Digestive system

Each of these energy forms has its own frequency and vibration. The cat's mental and emotional activities also produce energy. They all work in harmony and contribute to the cat's spiritual well-being, when there are no energetic blockages.

All interactions with our cats impact their energy, and it is really helpful if you can support your cat by allowing its energy to flow constantly. You have the capacity within you to affect your cat's energy with the words you use, your intention towards him/her and even with your own emotional state.

We are deeply connected with our cats, and because they are sensitive creatures, they can feel our energy, just as we can feel theirs.

As a cat guardian, have you ever looked at your cat and known something is wrong? You can't quite put your finger on it, you can't articulate it, but you just know. The reason you can't articulate it is because it's not a logical response; it's an energetic response. You can feel something is wrong or 'off' with your cat. These connections that you share with your cat will help to develop your energy-sensing skills. Trust them. Feel into them as we work through this book.

Energy is always moving, and to have a healthy state of balance and well-being, the energy needs to flow; it needs to move. Therefore, when energy becomes blocked or stagnant, it creates disease within the body. This will manifest as a behavioural response or a physical issue.

Blockages

Negative experiences, trauma or physical illness will compromise the body/mind/soul connection. If the physical body starts to present a physical symptom, there has been a blockage in the chakra for a while and it will need to be cleansed and rebalanced.

The blocked energy may be from a physical experience, such as physical abuse, or it could be from an emotional issue, such as abandonment.
These are extreme situations that can affect a chakra, but the truth is that even small changes in our cat's environment can impact its chakras and flow of energy.

Suppressing feelings or being unable to display normal cat behaviours can all impact the cat by creating congestion of energy, potentially leading to a blocked chakra.

It can be hard to detect which chakra is out of alignment if there are chronic issues but take comfort in the fact that you are attuned to the universal flow and you are able to help your cat. It may take more than one healing session, and you may need more than one support tool, but even by definition of having the intention to help the cat, you are making a positive difference to it.

Remember my experience of being on the sofa with Pickle? I didn't know what I was doing then; I hadn't had any training. I simply held the intention of helping her to heal. If I can do it, I know you can.
Intention is powerful.

It is important to understand that energetic healing is a process; it isn't an instant fix. While traditional treatments (Western medicine) can have almost immediate effects on physical symptoms, energetic healing has a softer, slower impact on the body as energetic integration takes time.

Consistent healing helps to maintain balance. It will help to shift energy to enable the body to heal itself and the energetic life force to find its unique rhythm and flow in the body again.

You may need more than one healing session with a cat to notice results, changes or improvements, but trust that the healing is working on a cellular, energetic level.

Keeping a notebook or journal when working with a cat can be really helpful. It enables you to make comparisons after each session, note where you have experienced changes in the cat's energy field and also see how far you've come in healing your feline friend.

Medication

Conventional, medical treatment won't always solve a physical issue with a cat; if the problem is chronic, energetic work may be needed to shift a blockage or remove an energy imbalance.

Don't forget that a physical issue or problem is a result of blocked or stagnant energy. While medication is largely used to treat a symptom, energetic work can help resolve the actual issue because energy is the key to healing, health and well-being.

There is huge debate regarding Western versus Eastern medicine, yet I believe there is no right or wrong, no one-size-fits-all way. As each cat is unique, its situation and energetic frequency are unique. Therefore, we need to be open to all treatment options and modalities.

The holistic approach to healing

A true holistic approach looks at the need of each cat, as an individual, and a treatment plan using more than one modality is likely to support the cat and ensure it is balanced and has a sense of well-being.

We were seeing a conventional vet for Pickle's diabetes management and when we weren't getting the results I wanted, I also started working with a homeopathic vet. That was when my true energy journey began. As he told me about the effects of Wi-Fi on Pickle's energy field, it blew my mind. I had never considered it before; I didn't realise it could impact her aura and chakras.

Medication can cause gaps in the auric field and affect the balance of the chakras. Cats on long-term medication will benefit from regular energy/healing sessions to support their chakras and the body while processing the effects of the medication.

It is unlikely that healing will interfere with medication by creating an adverse reaction, but in some instances, less medication may be required, such as with diabetes/insulin, as the body begins to heal itself.

Whenever Pickle had Reiki from me, I would be sure to check her glucose level and adjust her insulin dose accordingly.

Be prepared to monitor the cat after the healing session. It might be that the cat can come off certain medications if their body has reached a state of regulation and the medication is no longer needed to support the body's functions.

Not all vets will support complementary treatment options, but I would advise that you share with your vet that you are performing energy work with your cat.

A true holistic approach to our cat's health and well-being means all parties are informed of elements that may affect the cat and work together in a joined-up approach. This is also a valid reason for why healing/energy work needs to be conducted alongside conventional treatment.

You do not need your vet's permission to perform energy work with your cat yourself, as you are the cat's guardian and are entitled to treat it how you wish. However, should you use a qualified energy worker/practitioner to treat your cat, I recommend that you liaise with your vet beforehand.

Top Tip: Do not remove any prescribed medication from your cat without first consulting with your vet.

What is healing?

My personal belief is that healing can take many forms, and what is considered healing to one person may not be healing for another. That's why it is crucial to treat every cat as an individual, as a unique being like no other.

Healing means different things to different people.

In this book, I use the word 'healing' to signify the removal of blocked energy, balancing of energy centres and emotions, and an energy tool that helps the cat to find a sense of balance and peace. Essentially, it is helping the cat to achieve homeostasis, where the body can nurture and heal itself. The cat can be balanced and well.

My first experience of healing was with Pickle. We would lie on the sofa together with my hand on her tummy. We were struggling to get her diabetes stable at the time and had been back and forth to the vet's for nearly two years, yet she wasn't getting any better. She was still vomiting, poor coat, and displaying unpredictable behaviour.

As we lay together, I remember in that moment simply thinking over and over again: 'Help me heal her, help me heal her, help me heal her'. That thought occupied my focus. I was in surrender mode. I didn't know what else to do to help her.

After our cuddles, I checked her blood glucose level, and she was in the 'normal' range!
Something I had never seen since we had been managing her diabetes. And I'll be honest, a number I never saw again.

I didn't realise at the time that I was giving her healing; I was channelling the Universal energies through me to help her to heal. I had no training in energy work at this time, no courses, attunements, guidance or experience; I was simply a desperate mum, crying out for help to heal my baby girl.

And do you know what's truly amazing? We can ALL do this. You don't need a formal qualification or to be attuned to Reiki. Yes, it can help, but we are all divine beings of light able to connect to the energy around us.

Through this book, you will learn how to harness the energy of the Universe to heal your cat.

The aura

The aura is an energy field that surrounds a person or animal. It comprises seven energy layers, each with differing densities and frequencies, and each is connected to a chakra.

The aura surrounds the body like an eggshell around the whole body – top to toe (or paw!).
This 'layer' directly affects and influences the cat's physical well-being, mental capacity, emotional stability and spiritual clarity.

The aura extends about half a metre in each direction from the body and is an outward expression of what is happening within the internal, physical body.

The 'auric field' – as the aura is also known – is not usually visible to the naked eye. Although some energy practitioners can see it, but it can take years to master this ability. The easiest way to connect with an aura is to touch/sense/feel it.

As a cat guardian, you will have a heightened connection with your cat – more than any practitioner

– so you will be able to connect with your cat's aura easily.

You will be able to tell if its energy field is light/dark, heavy/fizzy, etc. I'm sure you have looked at your cat and thought, 'S/he just seems off'. That may be because you are reading the cat's body language, seeing the change in the brightness of its eyes, noticing a change in eating habits or a shift in its spirit or demeanour. But it is also because you can feel or sense your cat's energy.

Although this may not help when you have a vet appointment – 'I don't know what's wrong with her, she just seems off' – it really is your first step in connecting with your intuition, your inner knowing.

No one knows your cat better than you do.
The longer we have a cat, the more we are connected to it. Our love for the cat grows, and this creates and strengthens the energetic connection between us. It is this connection that is energetic.

The aura is a bubble of protection that maintains and protects the energy/life force. It is similar to the layers of the atmosphere around planet Earth. We need to cleanse and balance the aura (which is linked to the chakras) to prevent the auric field from being diminished.

The aura can be weakened by:

- Continued stress
- Medication
- Physical issues
- Changes in the environment
- Disease
- Poor nutrition
- Chemicals on the body or in the environment
- Changes in relationships
- Inability for the cat to act out normal cat behaviours.

The importance of nature

Regardless of whether you have an indoor or outdoor cat, nature is crucial in helping balance your cat's chakras and shifting the energy in its auric field.

If you have a cat that isn't allowed outside, it is really helpful to bring the outdoors indoors. Try setting up a sensory garden: bring in leaves, twigs, soil, grasses, and let your cat explore and connect with the elements. Having nature in a cat's environment will provide him/her with the mental and emotional support needed to enable it to balance its energies.

Or if you have capacity to create a safe, contained outdoor space, add natural elements such as cat-friendly grasses or plants, a soil playing box (like a child's sandpit) or a tree stump scratching post alongside the typical cat tree.

Tico enjoying the connection with nature.

Humans have the freedom to come and go where and when they please. We can get to a beach or visit the woods if we feel the need to connect with nature. Cats don't have the capacity to do that, so as their guardians we need to provide for them as best we can.

Bringing natural elements into the home, or ensuring the cat has access to them, is another way you can offer your cat the energetic support to help balance its chakras and aura.

Balancing the aura

Balancing the aura is a key part of energy medicine. It can be strengthened through:

- Colour therapy
- Nutrition
- Healing
- Crystals
- Applied zoopharmacognosy (self-selection)
- Sound therapy
- Mantras
- Nature
- Acupuncture/pressure
- Massage
- Homeopathy
- Meditation with the guardian

The layers of the aura overlap each other and will vary depending on the health, mental, emotional and physical state of the human or animal.

The aura is also affected by thoughts, feelings and emotions. Each layer vibrates on a specific frequency and is associated with a specific colour. Again, this aligns with the chakra system. If you are able to see an aura, you may see one dominant colour or possibly up to three or four different colours. As emotion and energy shifts, so does the auric field.

A breakdown of the aura

Layer	Emanates from	Distance from body	Colour
Etheric	Root chakra	1–5 cm	Red
Emotional	Sacral chakra	6–10 cm	Orange
Mental	Solar plexus chakra	10–15 cm	Yellow
Astral	Heart chakra	15–30 cm	Green
Etheric template	Throat chakra	30–60 cm	Blue
Celestial	Third eye chakra	80–90 cm	Indigo
Ketheric or causal	Crown chakra	1 m	Violet/white

In later chapters, I will share with you how to sense and feel your cat's auric field. Its aura can be like a map to an energetic imbalance. Therefore, if you feel a change of energy when stroking your cat's aura, it's likely they will need energy work to remove a blockage or to boost the flow of energy.

What is intuition and how can we use it?

Intuition is our connection to source/God/Universe, whichever word you feel comfortable using. It is our inner knowing, the true meaning of our soul, our connection to the Universe, and every single human has the capacity to tap into it.

Regardless of any religious beliefs you may have, ancient texts, scientific research and history show us that humans have the capacity for more than their 'humanness'. It is our internal guidance that leads us to what is needed for our highest good.

You know when you think of someone and they call you, or someone pops into your mind and you connect with them, and they share how much they needed you in that moment? That's your intuition guiding you. It's the spiritual connection that we all have with each other and with the Universe. It can be our guidance system if we listen to it.

As stated, everyone can connect to their intuition. It may take a little practice, but we can all be guided by something more than our logical brains.

As I introduced my new cat Baby Max to my existing cat, Leo, I had to consciously step out of my head and connect with my heart, my inner knowing, to know what to do next.

My training as a psychologist and behaviourist told me to introduce them a certain way: repeated exposure, desensitisation, breakdown of barriers, etc. But I'll be honest: my intuition led me down a very different route.

Instead of following the prescribed behaviour steps mentioned above, I introduced them slowly, taking my guidance from Leo and my intuition. When introducing cats to each other, you go at the pace of the slowest adjusting cat.

Leo set the pace for the integration and my intuition guided me in how to support him through this phase of change. I would experience my head saying, 'You need to do XX', then my intuition would give me a nudge that was 'Try it this way instead.' The more I trusted and followed that inner knowing, my intuition, the more progress we made with the two boys trusting and accepting each other.

Let's look at how you can be guided, what forms it takes and what kind of information you can get when you connect with and are guided by your intuition.

How to receive information

Just like day-to-day communication and interactions, each of us has a unique and preferred method of connecting, both with others and with our own intuition. For example, you may have heard people say they are visual learners, or they can't read a document – they prefer listening to the audiobook.

Well, connecting with our intuition, our inner knowing, and receiving messages is exactly the same. We will all have a dominant method of communication with our soul, and you don't need to know which yours is in order to access the information or connect with it. But you do need to trust what comes through to you.

It can be helpful to know which your default connection method is, but don't rule the others out! As your capacity to work with energy and your intuition grows, so will your skills and ability to receive.

Here are the main methods of communication from our intuition:

- Claircognizance – Clear knowing
- Clairaudience – Clear hearing
- Clairvoyant – Clear vision
- Clairgustance – Clear tasting
- Clairempathy – Clear emotion
- Clairsentience – Clear sense or feeling.

You are likely to experience more than one of these methods during a healing session, so trust what comes through.

It is **not** your imagination; it is your intuition. You **are** a healer; you **can** communicate with the cat and receive messages and information. Believe in your gifts. Believe in your connection. Believe in yourself.

I remember the first time I connected with my intuition, and it nearly knocked me off my feet. I was at an animal wildlife park, and as I walked past a large cat enclosure, I burst into tears. People thought I was mad! I later found out that the large cat had recently lost her mate; she was grieving. That's what I connected to: her energy, her sadness, her grief.

It was a true moment of awakening for me.

You may experience something similar when you start connecting with your cat's energy and emotions. Don't be afraid of what comes through, and don't question it.

To begin connecting with your intuition, start off simply. Our mind, the ego, can get very noisy very quickly, so in order to connect with yourself, it's important to just take a minute.

When we connect with our intuition, it may take a little practice. We need to quiet the mind by pausing or calming our thoughts and coming out of the logical head space to allow us to drop into the feeling heart space.

A simple way to connect to your intuition is to practise. I'd advise that you start by feeling what it's like in your body, and the easiest way to do this is to practise out loud. Let me explain.

Have you ever been to a restaurant and don't know what to order? You can't decide because you feel confused? You don't know what you fancy or what your body needs, and you think about what you had for tea last night and what you've got tomorrow. What then happens is that your mind starts to wander, and you think about jobs to do around the house, work emails, etc., and before you know it, the waiter/waitress comes back, and you are no closer to deciding what you want because you've been down a brain-led rabbit-hole!

The reason you get in that state is because you are *thinking* about what you want to eat rather than *feeling* it. Try this: speak your options out loud and notice how each makes you feel in your body.

'I am going to eat fish and chips.'
'I am going to eat the squash risotto.'

You will notice, albeit subtle to start with, physical changes in your body: your tummy tightens, your back slumps slightly and perhaps your pulse quickens. Or you feel a smile come across your face, your body lights up, loosens and you feel excited about receiving the food. This is our intuition – our body is showing us what we feel, rather than our brain telling us.

We can use our bodies to feel, to connect, to sense our intuition, our inner knowing. Sadly, a lot of the time we are in our heads, thinking rather than feeling.

If you need to strengthen your intuition 'muscle' or make that first connection with it, try the fish and chips/risotto test and notice what you feel. You can then increase your awareness and connection. It may be helpful to take a couple of deep breaths while doing this, and the section later in this book called

Calm Connection on page 141, is a very simple yet highly effective tool to help you come out of your head and drop into your heart.

Being in our heart space is where we are connected to our spirit – our soul – and where we can receive the guidance we need to heal our beloved feline friends – and ourselves.

What are chakras?

A diagram showing the approximate location of each of the seven main chakras.

'Chakra' comes from the Sanskrit word for 'wheel'. Each chakra stimulates a particular endocrine gland in the body to secrete a particular hormone. They are the very link between energy and matter, the spiritual and physical elements of the body.

Chakras are mainly controlled by emotions, which are affected by various internal factors, but they can also be affected by external factors such as the environment or human/animal relationships.

Chakras act as conductors for energy to move through the layers of the aura, from the environment and into the physical body. They are invisible energy centres that transmit energy between the cat's physical body, its aura and the environment. They act like a filtration system between a cat's energy, emotions, physical health and external environment. They unite all levels of 'being' for the cat. What they feel, experience and are exposed to will all affect their chakras.

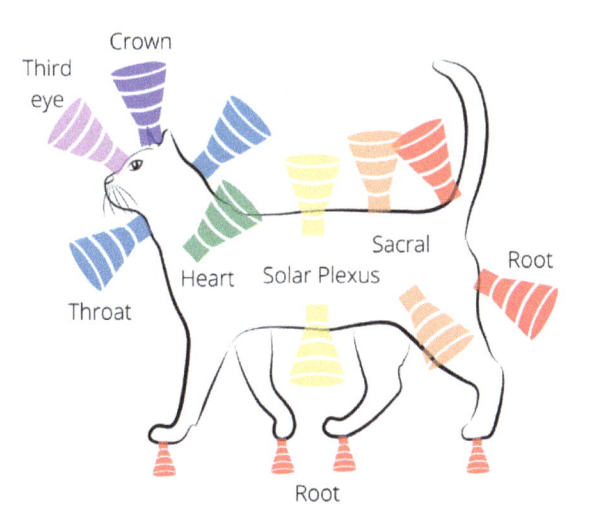

A diagram representing the cone like energy emanating from the chakras.

Chakras are not a single energy point in/around the body, rather they are like cones of energy that emanate from the body out into the aura, where the energy layers overlap and merge into each other.

This is why balancing one chakra will help a cat to some degree; even a small shift in energy will impact the whole. However, to achieve maximum wellness, all chakras need to be cleansed and balanced regularly to support the energetic needs of the cat.

At each chakra point, energy passes through from the auric field of energy bodies into one of the chakra points. We can see from the next image that the physical body is surrounded by energy and that each of these layers is connected.

A picture showing how the energy overlaps.

As mentioned at the start of this section, each chakra is connected with a specific gland in the body. When the energy/frequency of a certain chakra is not balanced, physical issues will present in the body. To maintain balance, health and wellness, the body/heart/mind/spirit connections need to be maintained.

The state of the chakras in our cats is crucial as their role is to manage the cat's energy, maintain physical health and support the cat in processing emotional trauma. All energy needs to move, and if a cat has what we call a 'blocked' chakra, it will eventually present with physical issues and symptoms.

Chakras are the storage centres for everything related to a cat's life experience. They contain energy related to their thoughts, emotions, feelings and experiences.

Each cat has its own unique vibration, which is created and affected by all elements that impact the cat. These include, but are not limited to:

- Age
- Diet
- Environment
- Animal relationships
- Human relationships
- Ability to express itself
- Socialisation experience
- Trauma.

When something happens to a cat, it will affect its vibration, its energy field. It may stimulate or sedate their chakras, causing an imbalance.

When we used to collect Pickle from the cattery (pre-diabetes), she would yowl. This yowling was her vocalising how stressful or unsettling the experience had been for her.

On reflection, I can now see why she would vomit more after being away from her home, her territory, her environment. Vomiting was one of the main symptoms we dealt with before she was diagnosed with diabetes. It was her body's way of sharing that she had issues and trying to show me that she had energy imbalances.

Just as an overactive chakra can be damaging, so can an underactive one. That is why energy healing and chakra balancing should be a key part of maintaining a cat's health and well-being.

The seven main chakras

There are seven main chakras in cats, although some schools of thought consider there to be more, which could include: Brachial, Sensing, Pad and Tail tip. Each acupressure point is also a minor chakra, helping to move the flow of energy in and out of the body. However, this book will focus on the seven main chakras.

Chakra	Location	Colour
Root	At the base of the tail	Red
Sacral	Above the hips	Orange
Solar plexus	Centre of the back, middle of the tummy	Yellow
Heart	In the middle, front of the chest	Green
Throat	At the throat	Blue
Third eye	In between the eyes	Indigo
Crown	Just above the top of the head, between the ears	Violet/white

You can use several methods to cleanse, clear and balance chakras. These include sound, light, crystals, essential oils, energy healing or flower/plant remedies. Clear quartz pointer crystals or wands contain all the colours of the rainbow, so they can heal any chakra, see the section 'Healing tools' on page 57 for more on crystals.

As you explore your cat's energy and your connection to the Universal healing energies, you will get to know which tools you and your cat prefer. Each cat is unique; each cat will process the energy differently.

Baby Max, for instance, loves his herb garden and will use it frequently, yet Leo is very rarely seen on it. Leo enjoys a hands-on healing session; he will usually lick himself clean when we start the session, settle down (looking as if he's asleep) during the session and then has a big stretch at the end to release the shifted energy.

Mirroring

Cats are known for mirroring our emotions and energy. In my experience, and according to many other healing/energy workers, cats have the capacity to heal us, but in order to do that, we need to understand what's going on.

Cats thrive on routine and are social creatures, but that's not all there is to see. Cats are extremely emotional, sensitive and loving. Yes, they are sensitive to changes in their environment, but they are even more sensitive to energy and frequency changes.

I'm sure we've all had an instance we can think of when we were poorly, and our cats came to sit with us (or on us!) When I had my wisdom teeth out, I was lying in bed and Pickle came up and literally sat on my shoulder, so she was leaning against my mouth – ouch! It was a little tender, but as she wasn't usually a lap cat, I wasn't going to let a little pain and discomfort stop me from having almost lap cuddles from her. I believe she was helping me to heal.

Never before, and never again, did she ever sit on my shoulder leaning against my jaw. You could call it a coincidence, but I believe she was healing me.

Cats help us to heal, and it's not only physical issues they can help with. Yes, the science is there to show that a) having a cat in our life is good for our health because of the frequency level of their purr and b) stroking them helps to soothe us, but
there is more.

Cats sense our energy, emotion and vibration. Remember how I mentioned that everything is made of energy? Well, cats can pick up on small changes in this energy.

I have seen first-hand how cats will exhibit a 'problem behaviour' with a root emotional cause that mirrors the guardian's current emotional state.
It is really common. They are here with us to help us heal.

For example, cats that are inappropriately urinating around the house are trying to communicate with us. Yes, it might be that the cat needs medical intervention if there is a physical issue such as urinary crystals, but equally, it could mean they have a blocked sacral chakra. We need to find time to listen to them as it could also be a nudge for us humans to connect to our intuition to discover the emotion that is sitting behind this behaviour from the cat.

The cat may have even started this 'problem behaviour' to encourage you to pause, to take time out, to reflect and re-connect with yourself, to lead you on a healing journey.

I've seen cats that are timid, shy and hiding away because so is the guardian – afraid to connect with others, afraid to let their magic be seen.

Cats are so powerful. As humans, we can get lost in our brains, so it can sometimes be easier to see a problem in others, i.e. our cats, than it is to see it in ourselves.

Cats will show us where we need to focus so we can learn and heal. That is the soul contract we made with all of the felines that come into our lives.

A soul contract is an agreement made between you and the cat before you came to Earth. It is an agreement that you will be together to benefit both your souls' growth and evolution. It is the reason this particular cat is with you, for the lessons they are here to teach you.

Energy and emotions

I remember when I went to a cat café for my birthday. I was really lucky as the café owner had brought in a bundle of kittens to give their hard-working mum a break.

They were adorable: all fluff and teeny tiny meeps. There was one kitten, in particular, and when I picked it up, my body seemed to come alive; my heart woke up. Even now I have trouble articulating what I felt. All I could say at the time was, 'I'm really drawn to this kitten'.

I had NO intention of getting a second cat at the time, but days later I could not get this kitten out of my thoughts. It made no logical sense for me to become a multi cat home, but something in me was desperate for him to be mine. I had a 'knowing', a feeling, and lo and behold, I am now guardian to my two cats Leo and Baby Max!

I believe that we had an energetic connection, a soul or spirit recognition because we have a soul contract together. Baby Max is here to help me, giving me more lessons. And can you believe it? He was born on the same date that Pickle was put to sleep two years previously. Coincidence, no?

We are taught to think, to be led by logic and reason, but this is only one way. When we understand how our interactions affect our cats, we can truly blossom and take our relationships with them to the next level.

This is also true of our emotions. I spent so much time being in fear with Pickle, worried about her health, worried about losing her, worried about treatment options. I didn't know then what I know now; I didn't know that my energy was affecting her. Now I try to be in a place of faith and trust. It's not always easy, but I'm trying.

When Leo didn't eat for six days one summer, I was a mess. He ended up being at the vet's for four days, on a drip and several medications. On the sixth day, I decided to step out of worry because there was literally nothing I could do to affect the situation. I wasn't with him; I couldn't make him eat and I had no control over what was going on. What I did have, though, was a choice.

My continuing worry started to make me unwell, and I remember thinking that I needed to be well for when my boy came home, so I moved into a state of surrender. That wasn't me not caring; it wasn't me giving up on him.

I decided to change my energy, my frequency. I started to think, 'He will eat when he's ready. Leo is a hungry boy. Leo thrives when he has food in his body. Leo is eating'. Within the hour, I got a call from the vet's to tell me he'd taken his first meal in days. That's how powerful energy work can be!

Cats respond well to energy because of their heightened sensitivity. With seven main energy systems that could break down, it's crucial that you know how to support their energetic needs. That's what we cover in Part 2 of this book.

Healing tools

There is a wide variety of additional tools you can use to balance, cleanse and clear your cat's chakras, alongside your energy work. There is no prescriptive answer about which tool is right for a particular cat in any particular moment; each tool or modality has its own merits.

When you connect with your intuition, your inner knowing, you may be guided to a particular tool. Remember, though, that it's important to ask your cat – after all, it is their healing session!

You may find what worked for you and your cat last time doesn't work the next, and that's okay. We humans don't always want a piece of chocolate to feel better; sometimes we want a relaxing massage or a walk outside in nature.

The lesson from your cat will be to be open and work with them to conduct the healing session. Let go of the need to be in control and allow your cat and your intuition to guide you to your next healing tool.

When I started working with essential oils, I remember I kept offering Pickle oils to help with her pain. I knew she was struggling with her joints, but she didn't select a single one! My frustration began to rise. I was desperate to help her, and I thought I knew what she needed. I took a step back and offered her my entire essential oil collection! She went straight to Geranium, which is a lovely balancing oil.

She wasn't ready to work on the physical pain in that moment; she needed more balancing before she could lean into her physical body.

This was my first lesson in letting the cat be the guide in a healing session. We don't know what our cats need; we can only offer them the tools to support their energetic needs. We then need to let them choose what they need in order to heal.

Your cat will help to guide you to the right tool in the moment. Be patient with yourself and take the time you need to connect with your cat and see what you are drawn to work with. If you have been offering frequent healing treatments and the cat seems to favour a particular tool, be sure to have it handy when you begin the session: you don't want your cat all chilled out and ready for healing when you haven't even brought its favourite crystal along! Be prepared.

Your cat may also show you they want healing when it feels inconvenient for you. There is a reason they want to connect with you in that particular moment, so support their needs as/when you can.

Cats don't really think; they feel. Some cats won't like to be around you if your head is full of noise or you are thinking about 101 things, as your energy will be frantic, stressed and dense.

An example of this is that Leo will frequently look for healing when I am running my evening bath before bedtime. This is a time that, as my day draws to a close, my energy will shift, and I will naturally come out of my head and drop more into my heart as I wind down.

I do have to keep an eye on the bath when Leo is ready for healing. Sometimes he will wait for me if I have to interrupt our session to stop the water, other times, not so much! Share with your cat what you can when you can.

In the next section, I give an overview of the tools you can use to support your cat's chakra to cleanse. Each topic can be expanded upon, so if you are drawn to specialise or go deeper into any one topic, be sure to check out the recommended reading section towards the end of the book.

As you know, we never stop learning. Let your cat and intuition guide you to your next chapter of growth.

Crystals

Crystal healing is a very wide topic, but we are solely focused here on how it applies to cat chakras.

Here are a few key points to note:

- All naturally made crystals affect energy and have their own unique vibration.
- Clear quartz is the most powerful crystal you can use because it contains all colour frequencies.
- Crystals need to be cleansed after each use.
- Crystals are powerful healing tools and need to be treated with respect.
- Crystals can be used to balance, charge and clear chakras.

Different crystals are thought to have different healing properties. If this interests you, you can read more about it in Part 2 of this book, where I have added information on a small selection of crystals that can support each chakra.

Note that I don't specify any particular shape for the crystal and that a tumble version of the crystal will suffice. (A tumble stone is a crystal that has been polished and had the edges rounded so it is smooth all over.)

Although you may have an idea of which crystal to use for your cat, be sure to ask their permission before you bring a crystal into their healing.

Some cats will enjoy having a crystal placed directly onto them to cleanse, clear or soothe a particular chakra. Ask the cat if this is what they need in the moment. Give them a choice.

Mitzie enjoying her crystal heart energies.

Other cats will be able to feel the vibration of the crystal with its simply being near them. Others may like to have the energy of the crystal 'filtered' before they receive it. This means you can hold the crystal in your hand while you work with the cat.

Ask the cat what it needs and trust in the answer you receive. If you aren't sure, don't use the crystal.
You can always put it on the floor/bed and if the cat needs to work with it, it will go and sit near/next to/on it, just like Mitzie in the picture.

Top Tip: Be sure to use big pieces of crystals to avoid the cat's accidentally swallowing them.

As the healing energy works through the cat, it may become playful and start to bat the crystal around. This might be to shift the cat's energy, or the energy stored in the crystal. Don't be tempted to tell your cat off – enjoy watching it play with the energy. It is all part of the healing session.

Crystals are vessels that store energy, so they need to be cleansed after every healing session. There are a variety of ways in which you can cleanse a crystal.

Simple methods include:

- In sunlight/moonlight/burying in soil
- Using sound
- Smudging
- Water
- Healing energy

Some crystals, such as selenite, don't react well to water, so be sure to read more on this topic. See the recommended reading section in the Appendices for crystal book recommendations.

To cleanse a crystal, you set the intention that you are clearing it of negative energy. For example, if you use water, you can run your crystal under the water flow while thinking inwardly or saying aloud the words: 'I cleanse this crystal of negative energy' three times. Or as you place the crystal into clean, turned-over soil, set the intention: 'I place you here to release and recharge'. You can leave your crystal in soil for 24 hours.

Smudging to cleanse crystals involves using sacred herbs or resins to create a cleansing smoke, so be sure to do it either outside or in a well-ventilated area. Don't do it immediately after a healing session as your cat may not react well to the scent or smoke.

Remedies

I have added a small selection of botanical remedies that can be offered to support each chakra, if needed. All remedies should be offered using self-selection.

Top Tip: NEVER force a remedy onto a cat; add it to food or apply it topically.

The remedy information given in this book is intended as a complement to the healing/energetic work and should be used under self-selection principles. More information on botanicals and self-selection can be found in my book, *The Aromatic Cat*. It details what self-selection is, how to use it with cats and how cats can benefit from the healing properties of essential oils, hydrosols, dried herbs and flowers.

Dried herbs and flowers are a great start to using self-selection with your cat. The energetic profile of the remedies is really subtle, and it is a lovely complement to the healing work. It supports the emotional release needed when balancing the chakras.

Herb gardens

Sepi, the cat in the picture, is enjoying a herb garden. A herb garden is when you place a towel, blanket or mat on the floor and add dried herbs and flowers.

Sepi healing with rose and calendula.

The mat should be in a quiet area of the home, away from a lot of foot traffic because cats need to feel safe and vulnerable to heal.

Add four dried flowers, one in each corner of the mat. Do not put more than four on the mat at any one time because it could overwhelm the cat. The scent molecules from the flowers could initiate a physical reaction in their body, such as reducing anxiety or calming their nervous system; the frequencies of the flowers will also help the cat to shift blocked or stored emotions.

By offering four at any one time, you are giving the cat the opportunity to heal in a balanced and measured way. You might find that a cat will sit with the herbs/flowers before they accept any direct healing work. Herbs help to open the cat up to healing.

Each cat will interact with the herb garden differently, exactly as they need to. Leo rarely uses our herb garden. If he does, it is usually overnight when no one else from the home is around or active! Baby Max, however, will rub/roll and generally mix up the herbs whenever he needs to.

There is no age limit to offering herbs; even younger cats will have energy they need to shift. This could be after leaving their mum and litter mates, coming to a new home or changing food.

I consider a herb garden an essential resource, just as important as a litter tray, because it is an emotional support tool for the cat. As cat guardians, we have a duty of care to provide for all their needs.

I have listed dried herbs and flowers that can be offered to support each chakra in Part 2.

Essential oils

When it comes to essential oils, they CAN be used safely with cats. Sadly, due to misuse, they have built a bad reputation for being used with cats and can be considered dangerous. This is not the case.

If you want to learn more about this, then my first book, *The Aromatic Cat*, explains why there have been negative stories about cats and essential oils and why misuse can cause issues. It also explains how essential oils can support a wide range of emotional, mental, physical and behavioural challenges with cats.

Ted, a three-legged cat, working with essential oils.

Essential oils are far more concentrated than dried herbs and flowers. That higher concentration means the cat may experience a deeper energy shift during its healing. Essential oils are a preferred healing tool over herbs and flowers if you have a cat that has a chronic issue or has experienced trauma such as physical abuse.

I don't encourage or support the use of diffusers in the home. This doesn't give the cat a choice in how they interact with the remedy as it puts the scent molecules into the atmosphere.

When using essential oils with cats, I would always recommend to either a) offer the bottle with the lid on to see if they select it or b) put a single drop of oil onto a piece of cotton fabric (I use a cut-up face cloth as it is very absorbent). Next, I place the piece of fabric on the floor for the cat to work with, if they choose to.

Some cats will work with the closed bottle of oil. After all, their sense of smell is phenomenal compared with us humans! They will also sense the energy of the oil from simply sitting with bottle.

Top Tip: Never leave your cat unattended with an open bottle of essential oil.

If you put pieces of fabric on the floor with an essential oil droplet on, make sure the pieces of fabric are large enough that the cat won't be able to eat them. Cats suffering from conditions such as Pica may like to lick at the fabric but will be unable to stop themselves from chewing at it. Although you can leave pieces of fabric down for your cat to use as and when they need to, if you have concerns around ingestion, don't leave your cat unattended.

Ingestion of the dried herbs and flowers is, however, considered safe as the cat's physical body can break down and process the components.

Colour/sound

Colour can be very supportive and nurturing for cats as it directly affects and impacts their chakras. I have added the colour associated with each chakra in Part 2.

You may receive feedback during a treatment that a cat would benefit from having a particular colour placed around the house, or a specific sound, like drumming, played for them. Trust what comes through your intuition.

Put coloured fabric pieces on the floor and let the cat choose to sit on or near such a colour. Do not add to existing beds or key sleeping spaces because you may disrupt the cat's 'normal' energetic spaces in the home.

In the image, you can see Baby Max positioning his body to balance his chakras. He isn't lying here by mistake; these pieces of fabric are laid across our spare bed, not somewhere Leo or Baby Max will regularly sleep. I see them both here as/when they need to use the frequency of the fabric.

Baby Max balancing his chakras across coloured fabric.

Bear in mind that although each colour is associated with a particular chakra, it doesn't mean the cat will only use that colour to heal itself. For example, red is usually associated with the root, but here we can see Baby Max is using the violet-coloured fabric. This is because the violet fabric has a higher frequency, which will stimulate his root more.

Colour therapy is a really simple and effective way to support your cat's energetic needs. Look at the colour of your cat's bed(s). Does your cat sleep in the bed? Perhaps it prefers the floor, a certain carpet or coloured sofa. Take note of the colours it leans towards and those it avoids – this will tell you which colour(s) it is working with and is another way you can gather information about your cat's energetic state. Have you ever bought your cat a new bed and they have never slept in it? It could be due to its colour, and therefore its frequency, which might feel detrimental to the cat's energetic state.

Colour therapy enables the cat to recharge or release energy from a particular chakra as and when needed. Remember that you don't know what the cat needs to heal, only it knows. You can help the cat by offering the seven main chakra colours for him/her to work with.

When you have several pieces of colour fabric around the home, you are likely to notice your cat rotating to sleep on different colours. They are using the colours to heal themselves. How fabulous is that?

I would recommend putting the pieces of fabric in and around the home for the cat to choose which it prefers to work with. You could also bring a selection of coloured fabrics to the healing session. I wouldn't recommend placing the fabric on or over the cat unless it guides you to do so. For some cats, it can feel restrictive and may impact their other energy centres. Let your cat be your guide. Let it show you what it needs. Give it a choice in its healing.

Mantras

Mantras are words or phrases that have meaning for you. They can be a tool used during meditation to focus the mind and breath and are commonly used to focus energy and intention. Indeed, some people have a particular statement of intention for their day ahead. Offering mantras to your cat can be a great way to focus your energy and offer them healing.

For example, when I did a chakra cleanse with a cat, she needed the words: 'You are loved. We see you' to support the energy integration from her treatment. Her guardians wrote the words on small, pink, heart-shaped post-it notes and put them around the small area where she liked to sleep.

Not only did they serve as a focal point for the cat's energy, but they also helped to serve as a reminder for the guardian when they approached the cat. They would say the words out loud and repeat them from their heart space, all in an effort to anchor in the cat's change of energy and to support its sense of balance and well-being.

There are mantras specific to each chakra in Part 2 and I have added a list of suggested mantras you can work with in the Appendices.

Explore how they feel for you, does any particular mantra resonate more for you? When you think of your cat, which one of the mantras I've offered feels aligned for you both? If you aren't sure which mantra to use you can work with a pendulum to get guidance.

Pendulum

A pendulum is usually a small weight, such as a crystal/bead or small ball suspended from a pivot, such as a chain or cord from which it can swing freely. It enables a person to ask questions and connect with their intuition. Usually, it is used for a Yes/No question. It can also shift/move and change energy. It is a tool that can support your connection with your intuition as it reacts as a transmitter and receiver of your energy.

My clear quartz pendulum.

The more you work with a pendulum, the more you will connect and attune to your intuition. It is a great tool to help you to trust what you receive when working with your cat. If you are just starting out and are stuck in the logical mind, a pendulum can be a really helpful tool.

There is no right or wrong way to work with a pendulum. But you do need to know what a 'Yes' response is and what a 'No' response is.

Start off by asking a simple question, such as 'Is my name XX?' and see which way it moves. Then ask a question to which you know the answer will be no, such as 'Am I male/female?' and see which way it moves.

Common responses to pendulum questions are:

- Moving clockwise/anticlockwise
- Swinging backwards/forwards
- Swinging side to side

This may sound simplistic, but it will tell you which way your pendulum will guide you. Some people may have clockwise for a yes and anticlockwise for a no.

Personally, as my logical mind can overcome my intuition, I need a very clear and distinctive response. My pendulum will show a circular motion for yes and a forward and backward motion for no!

Practise. Have fun with it. A pendulum will help you when you start to work with your cat and its energy. As you lean into and trust your intuition more and more, you may not feel the need to use the pendulum as much.

Top Tip: Don't let anyone touch or use your pendulum – attune it to your energy and keep it sacred.

When you are comfortable with how your pendulum is guiding you, practise, practise and practise some more! You can use your pendulum for anything – it is connected to the Universal energy, so will never misguide you.

When working with your cat and their chakras, you can use the pendulum to determine if it has a blockage, i.e. an under- or overactive chakra.

Be sure to ask simple questions and use the name of your cat:

- 'Is Leo's root chakra blocked?'
- 'Does Max have an underactive throat chakra?'
- 'Would Pickle benefit from a chakra balancing session?'

You can use the pendulum directly with your cat, for example, when sitting with him/her before you start a healing session. Or you can have a picture of the cat in front of you, or you can simply feel it. Connect to your love for the cat; think of something it did that made you smile. Connect to its essence, its frequency, and then ask the pendulum your questions.

Food

Nutrition is the foundation of health: what you put in; you get back out. I'm going to make a bold claim here: cats shouldn't have smelly poo!

In my 15+ years' experience working with and being a guardian of cats, they only have smelly poos when they are eating either a poor-quality diet or a species-inappropriate diet. Cats are obligate or 'true' carnivores: they need a mixture of meat/flesh, bones and organs to thrive. Think about a lion in the wild – they eat most of the antelope, from fur to heart and the gross bits in between.

I'll never forget when I was on holiday and heard a cat yowling, then an almighty crunch! I looked over my balcony to see one of the resident cats, Nala, enjoying her breakfast of a dead mouse.

Nala

I was mesmerised. I believe in a raw food diet for cats, so seeing it live and in action was enormously inspiring!

She ate the whole thing apart from a lung and a kidney. And yes, I took a picture as I was fascinated by her behaviour.

Sadly, man created dried cat food for human convenience. It is not a biologically appropriate food for our obligate carnivores, and they have not evolved to digest it and survive on it. Highly processed, dehydrated, chemical-covered, carbohydrate-based pieces do not enable a cat to thrive.

If your cat is fed dry food, I urge you to research a better quality, species-appropriate diet. If you can get your cat on to a high-quality wet food, it will really help to support its physical and energetic body.

If nutrition is poor, it can put unnecessary strain on the systems in the body. For example, a high-carbohydrate diet will put strain on the pancreas and, for cats, their kidneys. This will undoubtedly lead to energetic imbalances, possibly in more than one physical area, and chakra.

If switching diet feels overwhelming, try adding real food sources to your cat's diet to start with, such as egg (raw or scrambled), tinned fish in sunflower/olive oil or pieces of raw meat when preparing your human food. Take baby steps.

If you are comfortable offering a raw meat diet, good for you, that is the best you can do for your cat. It reflects a cat's natural diet the most. If it makes you a little uncomfortable, move to wet. Whatever you do, ditch the dry.

Animal communication

During a healing treatment, your spirit is open, your energy flowing and your heart space receiving. Trust what comes through for you.

Animal communication is a discipline in its own right; however, the premise of animal communication is closely linked to energy and healing work. You may find you're a natural animal communicator and receive additional information when working with a cat.

Just like you, the cat's energy is flowing, and its heart space is open. It may want to share messages, moments or thoughts with you. You may receive information from the cat in various forms, such as a thought, a smell or an image. Try not to overthink what you pick up and sense or feel from them. A soul-to-soul connection is really powerful and comes in various shapes and sizes, so to speak.

Making notes about anything you receive when working with your cat can be helpful. As mentioned in the earlier section on Mirroring, your cat may share with you something for your own growth and development. It's also really heart-warming to look back on previous sessions to see how your connection and relationship with your cat evolves and grows stronger.

At times, I struggle to connect to my own cats using animal communication. My logical brain takes over and my feelings turn to thoughts. When I started to connect with Leo, I actually wrote a letter to him. He was sitting in the summer room with me, asleep on a chair. I started to write him a letter to share how I was feeling, and before I realised it, the tense and tone of my writing had changed and the words I was writing were actually coming from him, not me.

Our logical brains can get in our way at times. We are conditioned to think, rather than feel, our way through life. When we ask for someone's opinion, we often say: 'What do you think?', not 'What do you feel about XX?'

There is a huge difference between thinking and feeling. When you start to work with energy, emotion and your intuition, you may find you need to practise coming out of your head and dropping into your heart. I know I do!

Our heart space, the heart chakra, is where our soul and spirit live. It's the home of our true connection to each other, and it is from this place that you are able to connect with your cat.

We cover how to prepare for a healing session in Part 2, and that includes how to prepare *you* for the session, too!

Meditation

Meditation is a technique used to focus a person's mind. It can be practised in many forms, including mindfulness, guided meditation and non-guided meditation. As a topic in its own right, you can research further into different forms of meditation if you wish.

I started using meditation to help me turn my thoughts off. My head would get so busy, getting lost in spirals of anxiety, and I needed a way to find a little peace of mind. I practise a mixture of guided and non-guided meditation, depending on what I need for that day.

One of the beautiful side effects I have noticed is that when I meditate, one or both of the boys will come and join me! I often get disturbed half-way through a practice session by a little furry friend climbing on to my legs, or I wake up to see one or both boys have settled with me in my meditation room.

Meditation changes our frequency and vibration, which our cats can feel. Not only is meditation known to reduce mental stress, it can also produce a calming effect on the body.

After reading this book, you might find that you'd like to start meditating. See if your cat will join you. Meditation is a great practice to help you come out of your busy, chaotic head and be more present with your body, surroundings and, ultimately, your cat.

Massage

Massage, at its core, is movement. It is a wonderful tool to stimulate the blood vessels, soothe muscles and relieve stiff joints.

In relation to chakra healing, it is fabulous at shifting energy. Energy is meant to flow, so when it doesn't, it creates a build-up of energy which, if not dealt with, will create a blockage. This blockage may present itself as tense/tight muscles or sore joints. The energy is literally being held – stored – in the physical body.

I bet you are already using massage with your cat. You know how they like chin rubs or cuddles, strokes or brushes. As I said before, no one knows your cat better than you.

But let me share this perspective with you – you are already using your inner knowing, your intuition, when you use physical touch with your cat. You may just not be consciously aware of it.

Have you ever had that moment when a family member comes to your home and goes to touch your cat and you cringe? You know that your cat doesn't like a hand straight in their face, or you know your cat needs to sniff first. You know your cat prefers soft, gentle strokes, not rushed, frantic contact.

You know this a) because you are an awesome cat guardian and b) because you are attuned to your cat's energy, so you know how they like it to flow.

Massage and physical touch can be another way to sense/feel and shift your cat's energy.

In my experience, a healthy, balanced chakra will spin clockwise. Therefore, you can use massage and physical touch to charge or reduce a cat's chakra by moving your hand in a clockwise or anticlockwise direction. You can do it just above the cat's physical body, in its auric field or on its physical body. Be gentle if you use the hands-on method of movement for your cat's energy; let him/her guide you as to how fast and how much is needed.

You may start off with just a finger or two moving the energy, or you may be guided to use your whole hand. Do what feels right.

Interestingly, Leo usually likes my whole hand when we share a healing session, whereas Baby Max, who is younger, likes my fingertips to be my healing tool. But this does vary for each session, so don't stick to one particular way to work with your cat. Be guided by what the cat needs in that session. You may find your cat puts a particular part of its body in or towards your hand for you to work with.

You will know when the energy work is done because either your cat will move away, or you will feel a change in the energy. For example, your hands may turn cold or the sensation in them will change.

As I discuss in Part 2, try to balance all chakras, if possible, rather than just working with one at any time. Covering all seven chakras will help your cat to feel more balanced and aligned.

Energy movement in the cat

Every cat is unique. Every chakra-clearing or balancing session will be unique. In the many years I have worked with cats, I have never had the same experience during a treatment. The more you work with a cat, the more you will get to know how they specifically process the healing and what their 'typical' signs of release are.

Our healing gifts are unique. Your experience of healing will be different with every cat, every time. You may notice that a session with a particular cat tends to go the same way as it has done previously, but as energy is always changing and expanding, we will never *feel* the same energy twice.

Therefore, although the cat may appear to have a 'pattern' of energy processing signals or signs, know that they will be processing the energy within their body and spirit differently from last time.

You do not control the energy; you simply enable its flow. You shift stagnant, blocked or sticky energy and bring through light, healing and high vibrational energy to each cat.

You are simply a tool, a mechanism to help the cat heal. You have no control over what it experiences, no say in how it should or should not react. You need to be prepared for any/all signs of energy shifting and processing.

Try not to enter into a healing session with any expectations. Be open to what might occur, being prepared for some of the more extreme reactions and holding the space for the cat to heal in exactly the way it needs to in that moment.

It can be quite upsetting if you see your cat start to hiss when you begin the healing work. Trust that your cat is working with the energy and releasing all it needs to. This is why setting the scene for a healing session is critical. There is more about this in Part 2.

Energy processing and energy release

There is a difference between energy processing and energy release.

In the tables that follow, I have listed signs of energy processing and signs of energetic release for the cat. They are in no particular order. It's important to familiarise yourself with these signals so you can be prepared during the treatment. Not every cat will display everything listed.

Energy processing is when the cat is shifting its energy. Perhaps it has a blocked chakra, which is when the energy cannot flow or move, causing it to become stagnant. Signs of energy processing are when the cat is moving the energy in its body through its chakra and out of its aura.

Cat responses to processing energy
Swallowing
Fur/body twitching
Trembling
Closing eyes/blinking

Cat responses to processing energy
Chirrup/meeping noises
Rolling and stretching
Lowering of the head/softening of the body
Laying down/stretching out
Hiccoughing
Stomach gurgling
Moving away/towards the healing
Slow/deep breathing/large exhale
Purring
Eyes flickering
Sleeping
Trance-like state
Taking themselves away from the family
Hiding/withdrawn
Change in appetite
Reluctance to physical touch

Energy release is when the stagnant energy has gained momentum or movement and is ready to be given back from the cat to the Universe. Essentially, letting go of the energy, releasing it from the blocked chakra back into the earth.

Cat responses to energy release
Hissing outburst
Deep sigh
Growling/howling/yowling
Crying/whimpering
Yawning
Cleaning activity
Sneezing
Passing wind
Irritable behaviour
Vomiting
Diarrhoea
Aggressive behaviour to other humans or animals in the home

When energy has been blocked for some time, it can be quite heavy on the cat's spirit and soul, making it hard to let it go. For example, blocked trauma will have a significant effect on the cat as it lets go of the emotions and everything associated with the trauma from its body and energy field.

In this instance, you may see a very reactive release such as hissing, or a deep yowling or crying. Do not be afraid. This is where you need to lean into faith and trust even more that you are helping your cat; it is doing what is needed to heal its body and soul.

Reactive releases don't usually happen every healing session. Once the 'bulk' of the stagnant energy has shifted, the cat will most likely display more subtle signs of energy processing and release.

In the following pictures, you can see how two cats experience the healing session differently. One is sitting in a very contained manner and the other is fully stretched out.

It doesn't mean that one cat is receiving more energy than the other or that one cat is healing more than the other.

Remember – there is no right or wrong way for the cat to process the healing energy; it is simply an example of healing for two different cats.

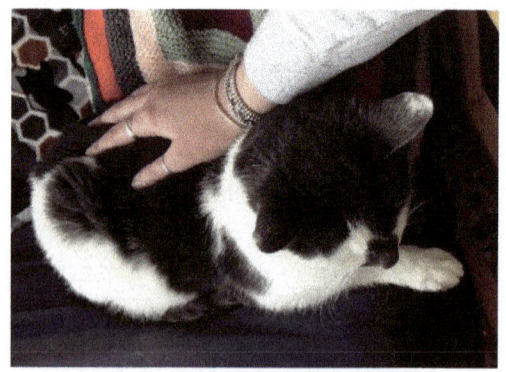

A very reserved rescue cat having hands on healing.

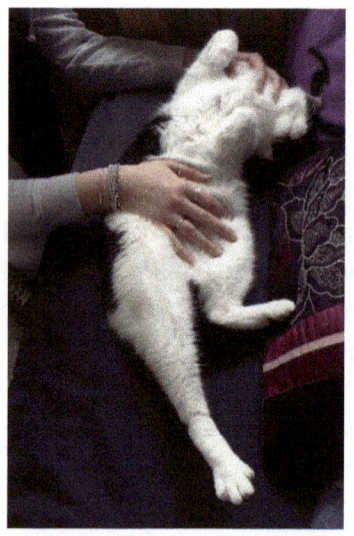

Another rescue cat stretching his body out to enjoy the healing.

Human responses to energy movement

When working with a cat to heal and balance its chakras, you are acting as an energetic conduit. It's crucial that you respect the energy you are working with by grounding and protecting yourself and the cat you are working with. The Universal energy moves *through* you; it shouldn't come *from* you. This is an important distinction to make.

You are not *giving* your energy to the cat; you are being a vessel for the energy to *move through you* for the cat. When you ground and protect your own energy you are keeping what's yours and embracing the opportunity to support the cat by connecting it with the Universal energy all around us.

You are enabling the cat to heal by directing the Universal to where the cat needs it most – their blocked or unbalanced chakras.

That said, when a human is involved in energy work, it will have an impact on them. I generally feel quite tired after working with a cat, being present, allowing the energy to flow through me, reading the cat, feeling the energy – it all takes effort.

When working with clients and their cats, I make sure I have breaks scheduled between appointments. Be sure to take this into account when you start to work with energy. I wouldn't advise sharing a healing treatment with your cat before going out for the day!

Be mindful of your own energy, as well as the cat's.

Energy isn't static, and as energetic beings we will be affected by energy that we come into contact with. Even if we are moving energy through us, it will affect us. That's why it is crucial to ground and protect your own energy when working with a cat, which is covered in Part 2.

When you are working with a cat, you may notice you experience some of the signs listed in the following table:

Human responses to energy movement	
Temperature changes to your hands/body	Pain in a particular part of your body
Tingling/popping sensation through your hands	Sensation under one finger or the palm of your hand
Drawing sensations from your hands into the cat	Tightening of a chakra space in your body
Warmth/cold	Bubbling

Human responses to energy movement	
Fizzing	Swallowing
Shivers	Yawning
Deep breaths	Tingling in your feet
Rumbling tummy	Twitches

Don't be surprised if you take and release a lot of deep breaths when working with a cat; you are a vessel to shift energy, so when you exhale you will automatically shift the energy in and around the cat.

I usually have some really big yawns when I am working with Leo. When I'm working with Baby Max, my temperature changes a lot between hot and cold.

If your healing gift is to sense energetic changes using Clairempathy (clear emotion) or Clairsentience (clear sense/feeling), you may feel, in yourself, an echo of what the cat is feeling or experiencing. For example, you may feel a tightening in your tummy or an ache in your foot, which is an example of Clairsentience. Or you may be overcome with a certain emotion that doesn't align with how you are experiencing the moment. Remember when I went to the Wildlife Park and suddenly burst into tears as I felt the grief of the large cat.

Be open to receiving *anything* when you are connected with your cat; cats are sentient beings, here to help us to grow, learn and evolve as beings of light and energy. Your cat may share with you messages, feelings, sensations or emotions when you are working together.

Try to release judgement, come out of the logical mind and head space and simply accept what the cat is sharing with you. Have a sense of gratitude and joy that you are able to receive all your cat is willing to share with you.

If needed, feel it and let it go, using a nice, deep exhale.

If you feel overwhelmed or uncomfortable when working with a cat and its energy centres, it's okay to pause, take a break and disconnect from the cat.

In Part 2, we look at how to conduct the healing session, set the scene for the cat and how to ground and protect your energy.

PART 2

The Chakra System

In this section, we will look at each of the chakras individually and how to use them to create and perform a healing session for your cat.

Be sure to take time to familiarise yourself with each of the chakras. If you read about how they present with imbalances, this will support your intuition when you start to connect with your cat's energy.

Behavioural changes are usually the first indication we have that a cat has an imbalance, so I have included an overview of which behaviours are linked to each energy centre for each chakra.

There is also an overview of supportive healing tools, such a crystals and remedies, that you can use to balance each of the seven chakras. Remember to offer the tools to your cat as they know what they need to heal.

Pictorial representations are provided for the location of each chakra but remember there is no single entry/exit point for the energy; it's more of a guideline as to where you can start to sense the energy.

Root Chakra – Muladhara

The square in the chakra symbol shows rigidity/stability and the downward-pointing arrow symbolises connection with Mother Earth, spirit connecting with matter. The triangle is the symbol for Earth, the circle shows it is all connected (infinity) and the four 'petals' represent the mind states: intellect, mind, consciousness and ego. *LAM* sound.

A grounded cat will feel established, part of the family or colony (feral) if they have a balanced root chakra.

Purpose: The root chakra connects the cat to the physical world. It is the starting point to work with when balancing the spiritual health of the cat. It is connected with the cat's survival instincts and drive, stability and security, logic and order. The root controls the flight/fight response. It is connected to the breath and represents the foundations for the cat. Being grounded, nourished and living in a stable and secure environment will help to balance the root.

It governs the cat's basic drives and its need to survive/thrive.

When engaging with your cat, take a deep breath and come into the moment. If you have capacity, visualise roots coming out from your cat's paws and going down into the earth. Or visualise a lovely, large oak tree and tie you both to the tree with a ribbon to help ground your body, mind, heart and soul.

Location: At the base of the spine, where the tail joins the body and at the soles of the feet.

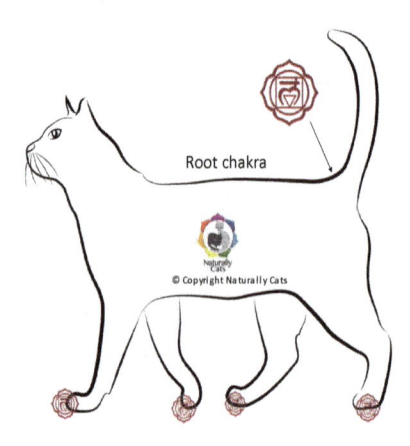

Root chakra

© Copyright Naturally Cats

In balance: When this chakra is in balance, the cat will appear content and confident. It will feel safe in its surroundings and be able to tolerate physical touch from humans. The cat will be able to build relationships with other animals and humans in the home.

It will display signs of thriving in its environment with continuous examples of trust and relationship building such as giving/accepting more physical touch or showing its tummy to you.

When the cat is grounded, it will be able to have an opening of the heart and connection of the spirit and soul. The cat will be able to exhibit 'normal' cat behaviours and have the capacity to represent itself by defending and confidently establishing territory.

Out of balance: If a cat's root chakra is out of balance, the cat will show signs of being excessively fearful, shut down and perhaps even trembling. It has gone into survival mode. It may appear withdrawn, detached and/or defensive, showing signs of being uninterested in human contact and connection. The cat will display an extreme flight reaction by hiding and may even display fear aggression behaviours as signs of anxiety.

There are likely to be problems with elimination and the cat may show a reduction in appetite as it leans into depression, lethargy, fatigue or lack of interest. In extreme cases, the cat may begin overgrooming as a need to control its environment and to self-soothe. It may also present with dandruff.

If the cat has a prolonged imbalance in the root, it will exhibit signs of a poor immune system. It will suffer emotional, mental and physical issues as it is out of balance and harmony with itself and its surroundings. The cat will be unable to connect with guardians or open up spiritually.

Examples of how the root chakra may become imbalanced: Being in a shelter/rescue centre. Being abandoned, abused, attacked (another animal or human). Being neglected, pushed aside from the family.

Left alone for long periods. Not taken care of. Needs not being met. Loss of personal power – territory, new cat, animal/human in the home.

Connection to physical body: Spine, bladder, colon, legs, feet, bones, large intestines, skin, immune system. Governs vitality.

Endocrine gland: Adrenal cortex.

Connection to emotional body: This chakra is connected to emotional and mental health. When this chakra is out of alignment, there is likely to be an emotional cause or mental health issue playing out as a self-destructive problem behaviour, such as overgrooming or fur pulling. It is connected to anger, frustration and aggression.

Connection to mental body: The root chakra governs stability. It is linked to the cat's ability to represent itself, defend its territory and feel established in the home. A sense of belonging.

Colour: Red.

Mantra: You are safe and secure.

Emotion: Fear/Trust.

Element: Earth.

Frequency (THz): 400–480.

Balancing: It is important to balance this chakra first as it grounds the spirit and soul, connecting the cat's physical body to the earthly plane. The root is where the cat will draw life force energy from.

If the cat isn't grounded or the root chakra balanced, you will not be able to balance the other chakras because you can't build on dodgy foundations! When the root chakra is balanced, the cat can let go of fear and move towards faith, trust and love.

If a cat has experienced trauma or a particularly traumatic event, it may need healing to help shift an energy blockage. It might not just be a case of balancing the chakra. Healing may be needed first to enable the energy to flow and balance to be found.

What can help to balance the root?

Play and physical movement, which builds trust and promotes joy. Being connected with nature. Catio (outdoor enclosure)/harness/sensory garden for indoor cats.
Blood – raw food or treats added to existing food or as a supplement. Established and defined territory. Routine and consistency.

Crystals: Garnet, smoky quartz, red jasper, bloodstone, ruby, black obsidian.

Essential oils: Sandalwood, frankincense, ginger, vetiver, pink lotus, angelica, jasmine, geranium.

Dried herbs: Valerian root, angelica root, ginger root.

Sacral Chakra – Svadhisthana

The circles represent the phases of the moon and the close relationship between water and our emotions. Birth/Death/Re-birth. The number of petals increases as the energy flow increases. *VAM* sound.

Purpose: The sacral chakra is linked to the cat's sense of identity. If a cat is prevented from displaying 'normal' cat behaviours, it may develop a blockage here. Understanding and appreciating the uniqueness of your cat is crucial to supporting its sacral chakra.

It is advisable to check the state of this chakra if the cat has been neutered. If the cat was previously part of a breeding programme, it is likely to be blocked or heavily out of balance.

This is a wonderful chakra to use to connect with your cat. Having focused playtime together will help you to bond. Turning off distractions such as devices so you can be present with your cat in the moment, will help to open both of your sacral chakras.

Look at your expectations of your cat. If you feel it should be a certain way, this projection of expectation will reduce the energy in its sacral chakra. Understanding the particular ways your cat likes to live, express itself and show you love is essential when it comes to the health of its sacral chakra.

Location: Above the hips – towards the end of the spine.

In balance: When a cat has a balanced sacral chakra, it will be joyful, flexible, adaptive and playful; it will engage in play with humans and other animals. It will show signs of being confident and at ease in itself and its surroundings. It may even display 'kitten'-like behaviours, regardless of its age.

Out of balance: Overly emotional, excessive vocalisation. Lack of boundaries. On edge. Restless. Low energy. Lack of confidence. Urinary issues.
Inappropriate urination around the home or outside of the litter tray. Jealous of other animals in the home. Unfocused. Over-eating. Asthma, allergies. Light sleeper.

Examples of how the sacral chakra may become imbalanced: The sacral chakra is commonly imbalanced in cats living in a multi-cat home due to the overlapping territory, diminished time with the guardian and comparison with other cats. As the sacral chakra is connected to boundaries and a sense of self in the home, it can be imbalanced through bullying from other cats or dominant humans.

Extreme evidence of overactive sacral would be overgrooming to fulfil the need for the cat to control something in its sphere. It may be particularly difficult to stop the overgrooming, and a fiercely regimented daily routine would be needed to provide structure and comfort.

Connection to physical body: Sexual organs, pelvis, bladder, stomach, kidneys, circulatory system, small intestines.

Endocrine gland: Ovaries/testes.

Connection to emotional body: Not as heavily linked to Yin/Yang, male/female duality in cats as it is for humans, for cats don't align with one sex more than the other.

Although this chakra in cats is linked to pleasure, a cat's pleasure tends to come from engagement with humans, good nutrition and environment enrichment. It's more about expression of the individual for cats.

Connection to mental body: This chakra is connected to relationships and an element of control over the external environment. Cats that have a lack of autonomy over their territory will have issues with this chakra.

Colour: Orange.

Mantra: You can feel joy and allow peace to flow through you.

Emotion: Control/autonomy.

Element: Water.

Frequency (THz): 480–510.

Balancing: This chakra is heavily connected to the root, which is the one responsible for stability. As mentioned, it is crucial to ground the cat before you begin to work on this chakra. Be slow and steady with energy removal/balancing.

This chakra is also connected to the solar plexus (the emotional powerhouse), so you may notice extreme or reactive emotional outbursts when clearing the energy.

What can help to balance the sacral chakra?

Choice. Clear, concise, regular daily structure. Timed feeding. Routine. Autonomy. Brushing – this is a fantastic bonding activity. When used, it can offer the cat the choice of leaning into the relationship-bonding exercise with a human. It can also help to reduce overgrooming behaviours.

Multiple resources for a multi-cat home. Be sure to notice what each cat needs such as: height/levels/hiding/quiet time/engagement, etc.

A cat with a regularly blocked/under-/overactive sacral chakra needs more stability and autonomy in its territory and external environment.

Crystals: Agate, tiger's eye, carnelian, garnet, orange jasper, calcite.

Essential oils: Neroli, ylang ylang, cinnamon, rosemary, orange, mandarin, melissa.

Dried herbs: Violet leaf, catnip leaf, calendula flowers.

Solar Plexus Chakra – Manipura

The triangle represents a funnel of energy moving upwards and is the fire sign; it is surrounded by the circle, representing the whole of creation. The number of petals increases in the chakras as the energy and awareness increase. *RAM* sound.

Purpose: The solar plexus chakra is the cat's source of power and emotions. It is where its sense of balance for self-confidence and self-control sits.

Sensitivity and self-esteem emanate from this chakra. If a cat has previously suffered trauma, it is likely to need support in this chakra.

It may take time to heal any wounds or trauma held in this chakra. Many domesticated cats can be depleted in this area as humans have so much control over their environment and expectations of how the cat should behave. As cats are so sensitive, they can sense and feel our emotions; some cats will store those in this chakra. It is essential to ensure that the cat has ways to express and release its emotions to prevent blockages here.

Location: Centre of the back and middle of the tummy.

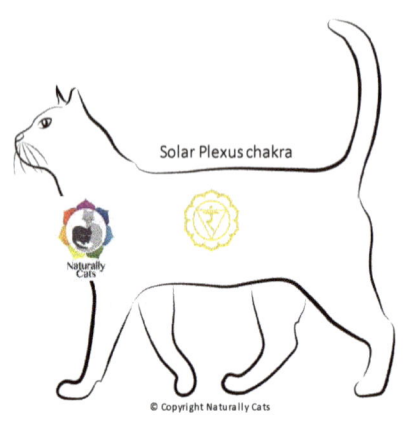

In balance: When a cat's solar plexus chakra is balanced, it will be confident and happy. This may look different for each cat, but essentially it is content in who it is and how it shifts its emotions. The cat would be open to having new experiences and, potentially, be bold in play behaviours.

It would demonstrate signs of being a good hunter, regardless of indoor or outdoor activity. The cat would display an even balance of play and sleep activity. It would have a clean, well-maintained coat along with a balanced appetite. It would be emotionally steady and secure enough to handle changes to its routine or environment.

Out of balance: Digestive upset – eating too much or not enough. Immune issues. Withdrawn – lack of motivation to play or engage with its surroundings.

Will not react well to control or being 'caged'. May show aggressive behaviours or be overly timid – out of character for the particular cat.

Pacing can be a sign that the cat is trying to shift its emotions and the energy of the solar plexus, which can lead to the cat being restless. It is literally trying to move the energy as it walks.

Some cats may have occasional vomiting if they have excessive energy in their solar plexus. They will be unable to 'stomach' any more emotions, so will not be able to digest food efficiently.

Examples of how the solar plexus chakra may become imbalanced: If the cat is used in a co-dependent relationship with the human and has no emotional release tools, it can lead to a blocked solar plexus.

Colour therapy or herb gardens are great options to offer the cat to enable it to shift the energy that has formed from emotions in its solar plexus.

We also need to be mindful that because our cats pick up on our energy and emotions, we need to take care and nurture our own emotional and energetic health to reduce the impact it can have on our cats.

Excessive emotions in the environment will impact the solar plexus. For example, if there is a lot of arguing, sorrow or abuse between others in the home, the cat will be acting like an energetic sponge and absorbing the energy to try to heal and help the humans.

Connection to physical body: Stomach, gallbladder, liver, diaphragm, nervous system.

Endocrine gland: Pancreas.

Connection to emotional body: Self-worth and confidence. The cat will feel established in who it is when this chakra is balanced. It will display its own unique and possibly 'quirky' ways to connect with humans and other animals in the home.

Connection to mental body: Personal power centre. Culmination of the previous two chakras regarding sense of self, control and individuality. Linked to the cat's ability to look after itself. Inner spirit.

Colour: Yellow.

Mantra: You are powerful and strong.

Emotion: Power.

Element: Fire.

Frequency (THz): 510–530.

Balancing: As this chakra sits in the middle of the physical body, you can align, balance and clear this chakra on its own. However, it would be more effective to balance the chakras below it first as they feed into this one.

What can help to balance the solar plexus chakra?

Quiet time, deep connection, play, celebration of the cat's uniqueness. Tending to your own energetic health will directly impact your cat's solar plexus. If you need motivation to meditate, get out for that walk or create journal time, look to your furry friend! By helping yourself, you will be helping your cat.

Crystals: Amber, yellow topaz, citrine, yellow calcite, sulphur, fire opal, yellow sapphire.

Essential oils: Chamomile, bergamot, frankincense, geranium, ginger, lemongrass.

Dried herbs: Calendula flowers, chamomile flowers, yarrow flowers.

Heart Chakra – Anahata

The two triangles represent 'funnels' of energy as the heart links the physical and spiritual chakras. Each triangle is thought to represent the combining of the male and female energies. The combination of the star points and the petals symbolises the 72,000 energy channels into the body. *YAM* sound.

Purpose: The heart chakra connects the top and bottom chakras. It is the key chakra to connect the body, mind and soul to the heart (physical). It is the source of love and acceptance for the cat.

A lot of cats are connected to their humans via their heart chakra. It represents how they connect as a soul being to other animals, human and non-human. It is an integral point to align all chakras and energy sources, which is why it can be balanced on its own. The heart chakra is the key to the cat's spiritual balance, sense of love and peace.

Cats are truly present beings: they live from their heart space day to day. The heart chakra enables them to feel love, connection and is the key to how they thrive.

Location: In the middle at the front of their chest.

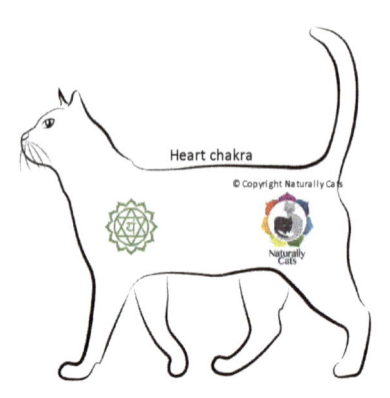

In balance: When the cat's heart chakra is in balance, it will display all the signs of a happy cat! It will be connected with its guardian, being able to give and receive love. It will show signs of being content, with literally a visible smile on its face. The cat will show relaxed features, have a soft coat and good appetite. It may even play with its food or show signs of silliness. It will be interested in play, making the human laugh. The cat will have the ability to heal itself and the humans.

Out of balance: Defensive aggression, unable to tolerate touch or interaction. Sadness. Lack of personality. No motivation to engage. Irregular heartbeat, immune issues. Lung infections, high blood pressure. Yowling or stifled cries. Unkempt coat. Lack of movement, inactive. Sleeping lots/more. Pacing at night. Restlessness. Inability to bond. Aggression. Attacking.

Examples of how the heart chakra may become imbalanced: Lack of love, trauma, neglect, abuse, lack of connection, abandonment, betrayal, bitterness/anger from human directed towards the cat.

Connection to physical body: Heart. Blood circulation. Lungs. Lymphatic system.

Endocrine gland: Thymus.

Connection to emotional body: Balance of this chakra is key; it will determine mental, physical and emotional health. This chakra IS the emotional/mental connection. A cat with a balanced heart chakra is able to give and receiving love.

Connection to mental body: Attitudes of happiness, joy, love, acceptance, peace. Confident to open their heart and spirit to connect with others.

Colour: Green/pink.

Mantra: You are loved, held and supported.

Emotion: Love.

Element: Air.

Frequency (THz): 530–580.

Balancing: Can be balanced as a stand-alone chakra. Using clear quartz on this chakra will help to shift blocked energy in other chakras. Can be used as a 'quick' form of healing. Ensure it is protected and aligned as it affects the other chakra points.

What can help to balance the heart chakra?

Energy healing, connection such as play or brushing. Love – in its simplest form. Nurturing of the cat's needs.

Crystals: Rose quartz, jade, peridot, malachite, emerald, green tourmaline, green calcite.

Essential oils: Rose, lavender, jasmine, angelica, geranium.

Dried herbs: Rosebuds, jasmine flowers, angelica root, lemon balm leaf.

Throat Chakra – Vishuddha

The triangle represents the funnel of energy from the heart moving up towards the higher spirit chakras. Associated with the element of ether. The petals are connected to the 16 vowels of Sanskrit. *HAM* sound.

Purpose: The throat chakra is the first of the three spiritual centres, the top three chakras. It influences the cat's ability to communicate, being the source of verbal, spiritual and emotional expression. It connects the body to the mind and is linked to balance and communication.

Location: At their throat.

Throat chakra

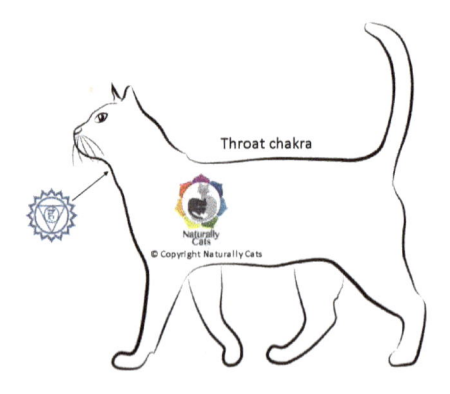

In balance: The throat chakra is one of the easiest to monitor in your cat. Every cat has its own vocal range. Meeps, peeps, purrs, meows, cries, yowls, howls. Only you know how your cat expresses itself. Some cats won't 'talk' very much, while others will have very distinctive and distinguished communication.

It's not just about the frequency or volume of your cat's communication with you that indicates the health of their throat chakra. It's about how it changes, and this will differ for every cat.

For example, Baby Max becomes quite vocal when he is happy or proud. When he brings a mouse into the house, he announces it to me! Yet Leo isn't very vocal at all, so when he yowls, I know something isn't right.

A balanced appetite and good grooming schedule/practice are also signs of a balanced throat chakra.

Out of balance: This chakra can be easily identified as being out of balance because your cat's vocal communication will have changed. It may become excessively vocal or lose its voice. You may notice destructive chewing or the eating of strange items that occurs suddenly. It may also start vomiting if the chakra is blocked.

The cat may become timid and will most certainly have teeth and or gum issues, such as inflammation. It may also demonstrate a dry cough coming from the throat rather than the chest/lungs. Its appetite will be impacted, so look out for a sudden change of either eating food slowly or bolting it down. There will be a lack of grooming and possibly shoulder pain or sensitivity to touch in this area.

Examples of how the throat chakra may become imbalanced: Being shouted at by a human will diminish the energy in the throat chakra. Although we all get frustrated or overwhelmed at times and snap at our cat, continued expression of frustration from us will eventually cause a blockage in the throat chakra.

For example, if the cat keeps scratching the side of the sofa or urinating outside the litter tray, we need to take the time to try and understand this behaviour. Shouting at the cat or expressing our frustration and anger will not enable a smooth flow of energy in the throat for the cat.

Reduction in territory leading to the cat being unable to express itself will also impact the energy in the throat. Expression and communication aren't just in terms of vocalisation; the cat must be able to mark its territory, create and set boundaries and show love to enable the throat to thrive.

Connection to physical body: Throat, neck, parathyroid glands, jaw, mouth and tongue. Respiratory system.

Endocrine gland: Thyroid.

Connection to emotional body: The voice represents the cat's ability to share and show who it is and what it needs. It provides the cat a medium to express itself.

Environmental stimulation is critical for enabling the emotional side of this chakra to be in balance.
If the cat does not have the crucial resources to thrive, it is likely to develop a block in this chakra.

Each cat is unique, and the understanding AND acceptance of this from humans will impact this chakra.

Connection to mental body: Capacity for self-expression and communication with others. Expressing their truth, showing who they are as a cat, is the key to the balance of this chakra.

Colour: Blue.

Mantra: You can use your voice to connect with others.

Emotion: Truth.

Element: The ethers.

Frequency (THz): 580–675.

Balancing: The cat needs to be heard. Whatever the change in its communication with you (excessively verbal or more withdrawn), it needs to be received, heard. Take time out. Turn off distractions. Hear your cat. See your cat. Be present with your cat. Allow it the space to communicate with you and you will shift the energy in its chakra.

Meditation can be a great tool here if you need support to quiet your mind and open your heart to receive your cat.

Do not overcharge the throat chakra, as it can lead to excessive vocalisation. When balancing this chakra, watch the cat's body language. If he/she moves its neck or head slightly away from your hands, it is indicating that it has enough energy in this chakra. Do not continue to charge it.

What can help to balance the throat chakra?

Offering the cat a mantra, either on a piece of paper or offering the words into the energy of the throat chakra, can help. There is a list of suggested mantras you can offer in the Appendices.

Talk to your cat: using words with a loving tone can be very supportive and balancing for it. Despite the situation, words have power. They are energy in themselves. Tell your cat how you feel, what you want, how you are trying to help them.

We can shift energy when we vocalise emotions. Think about the flow of energy – it emanates from the solar plexus (the powerhouse of emotions), comes up through the heart (the centre of love and connection) and then needs to come out.

If your cat is displaying behaviours you don't like or understand, communicate with him/her energetically, emotionally or verbally. Make that connection with the cat and make space to receive it. Being present and quiet with your cat will allow it to communicate with you.

Crystals: Turquoise, sapphire, lapis lazuli, blue topaz, angelite, blue calcite.

Essential oils: German chamomile, nettle (powder), peppermint, spearmint, lemon.

Dried herbs: Chickweed leaf, ginger root, peppermint leaf.

Third Eye Chakra – Ajna

Associated with the dimension of light. Two petals symbolise the duality between the cat and the Universe or, as some think, the body and spirit. Funnel/arrow continues the flow of energy and awareness up to the crown. *OM* sound.

Purpose: The third eye chakra represents spiritual connection in cats. It is the link between their physical body and spiritual awareness (heart/head/spirit). This chakra is where the cat's soul contract with the human is held.

The third eye also releases negative, repressed thoughts and emotions that have moved up from the solar plexus. It is the spiritual connection to past life experiences and soul connections. There is an invisible silver cord from the third eye that connects the cat with a human.

Location: In between the cat's eyes at the brow point.

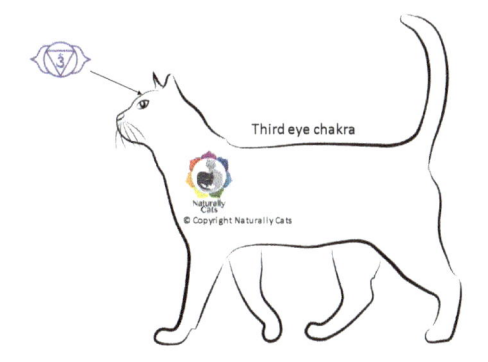

In balance: When a cat's third eye chakra is in balance, its sense of intuition is heightened and active. It will follow or anticipate where you are/where you are going. When you think of your cat, it will appear. If your psychic connection is strong, you can 'call' for it using your third eye, and it will hear you.

You might be able to hear/feel what it is thinking. The cat will demonstrate a balanced level of awake and sleeping, have a healthy appetite and present with no teeth, gum or ear issues.

Out of balance: Headaches – demonstrated by hiding in the darkness. Eye discharge or issues. Concentration issues. Hearing issues or discharge. Skin allergies. Distant. Unconnected. Withdrawn.

Depression/hyperactivity. Unable to settle or find comfort. Change in behaviours, mood swings. Retreating type physical behaviour. Reluctance for physical touch. Lack of emotional connection to humans. Lack of coordination. Unsettled sleep pattern, disturbed sleep.

Examples of how the third eye chakra may become imbalanced: Rejection. Lack of connection with the human. The human not being open to the spiritual connection with the cat.

Connection to physical body: Brain, eyes, ears.

Endocrine gland: Pituitary.

Connection to emotional body: Focal point of intuition and emotions, which cats use for connection. This chakra is the tether to the spiritual bodies. It is their link to energy awareness.

Connection to mental body:

The third eye chakra is the connection between the emotional and mental bodies. The cat needs to be able to express its emotions to have a balanced mental body for this chakra.

Colour: Indigo.

Mantra: You can trust yourself and be exactly who you are.

Emotion: Connection.

Element: The Universe.

Frequency (THz): 675–700.

Balancing: Slow, soft strokes of the space in between the eyes, moving from the eyes up towards the body. Moving the flow of energy. Quiet time with the cat. Meditation together. The more you embrace and honour your gifts, the more balanced the cat's third eye will become.

What can help to balance the third eye chakra?
Music, healing, guardian interaction and joint meditation. Energy clearing in the home. Grounding of energy. Tenderness.

Crystals: Purple fluorite, blue sapphire, sodalite, tanzanite, blue lace agate.

Essential oils: Bay laurel, clary sage, marjoram, vetiver, violet leaf, yarrow.

Dried herbs: Yarrow, lemongrass leaf, St John's Wort, linden blossom.

Crown Chakra – Sahaswara

Flower of a thousand petals – symbolises the interconnectedness of each other/every being. The circle represents the cyclical nature of life. *OM* sound.

Purpose: The crown chakra governs the release of Karma and is the connection to the higher realms. For a cat, this chakra is how it is connected to the Universe. Its spiritual energy flows in through this chakra.

Cat's crown chakras are usually very active as they are sensitive beings deeply connected to Universal energies. Younger cats will have a very active crown chakra as they settle into their body in this realm. Older cats may have an imbalanced crown chakra as they are more present in their physical bodies, dealing with aches and pains.

Location: Just above the top of their head, in between their ears.

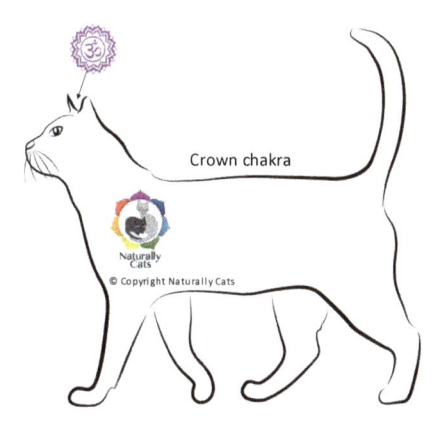

Crown chakra

In balance: A happy, well-adjusted cat with a good appetite. Adapts to changes in its environment easily, shows its unique personality, connects with other animals and humans. Sleeps well, engages in play activity. Good physical condition and emotional/mental health. Deep connection to the human.

Out of balance: Mental illness, slow/stiff body movements. Sensitivity to light, sounds or certain environmental stimuli.
Coordination issues, forgetfulness. Trouble being grounded, confused. Skin irritations, allergies, infections, hyperesthesia of the spine.

Examples of how the crown chakra may become imbalanced: Common to be out of balance in elderly cats, who can become absorbed in their physical bodies.

Likely to be out of balance if there are chronic physical issues. Abuse. Cat becomes stuck in the stimulation of their environment and can't connect to themselves. Fight/Flight/Freeze is very pronounced and consistent.

Connection to physical body: Skin, joint connections, central nervous system, muscular system.

Endocrine gland: Pineal.

Connection to emotional body: Source of prana/Qui life force energy.

Connection to mental body: This chakra connects the physical, mental and spiritual bodies. When the cat is balanced, healthy and well, it will be able to connect with and open this chakra.

Colour: Violet/White.

Mantra: You are love, light and joy. I see you.

Emotion: Joy.

Element: The Cosmos.

Frequency (THz): 700–790.

Balancing: Crucial to be balanced in accordance with the other chakras. Only charge this chakra as much as the spirit allows. Needs to be balanced along with the root chakra.

What can help to balance the crown chakra?
All forms of healing, crystals, light/colour healing, Reiki. Play, unconditional love, acceptance, appreciation.

Crystals: Amethyst, selenite, diamond, white calcite, opal, moonstone.

Essential oils: Jasmine, rose, geranium, sandalwood, frankincense, spikenard, vetiver, hemp.

Dried herbs: Hops, rose, valerian root, lemon balm leaf.

How to manage energy

When you are working with energy, it essential to manage that energy – to respect and direct it. Because energy overlaps and is not contained in a single space, you need to be clear, using your intention where you are directing the energy. You don't want to give your cat your energy or take from its.

Whether you are working with your cat in physical form or using a picture of it, you still need to be aware of directing the energy you are working with.

When I first started chakra cleanses with Leo, I would use a photograph of him rather than sitting with him in person. This was so that I didn't get distracted by his behaviour. My mind wasn't allowed to start interpreting his movement and physical form, leading to me becoming lost in my thoughts. It gave me the opportunity to connect more with my intuition and heart space.

You may find it easier to start with a photo of your cat when you are sensing its energy. Working with a cat remotely (via a picture) is a great way to offer energetic support to cats who are perhaps not comfortable with human interaction. These can include cats at a rescue centre or in another part of the world.

Energy has no limits; it is not constrained by continents! When you are able to receive energy, to find the frequency of a cat, you will be able to help many. The healing tools, techniques and chakra information in this book can be applied to a physical cat sitting in front of you or simply a photo of it. Either way, be open to receiving and being guided by your intuition. If you are leading from your heart space, you can't get it wrong.

Grounding and protecting are two simple, effective, powerful ways to manage energy. Both can be done using various methods, such as a simple moment of intention or through a longer meditation practice.

Remember, energy flows in, around and through us. When you ground and protect your own energy and your cat's, it enables the energy to remain with that being, aligning with its individual frequency for its own health and well-being to help, heal and make whole.

What is grounding?

Grounding is when the body – cat or human – has direct contact with the earth or ground. Some people believe it is only really effective when the feet are touching grass or another form of nature, such as a forest floor. I believe that even being on a carpeted floor can help to ground a cat, and when we use our intention to ground its energy, this can be more powerful than actual touch or contact.

Energy carries its own frequency and charge and as mentioned, it needs to flow. When the cat is connected to the earth, the energy can flow to or from the earth into, around and through the cat.

When a soul or spirit is 'ungrounded', it means that the energetic connection between the being and the earth is either light, low or non-existent. Physical bodies need to be anchored. When the being is grounded, the energy has a greater chance to flow and heal.

Grounding is needed before and after a chakra cleanse with a cat to support the transition of energy.

What is protecting?

Protection has many definitions when it's aligned with energy in the spiritual world. For this book, we are talking about protecting energy that has been balanced, cleansed or healed.

When you have spent time performing a chakra cleanse on your cat, it is important to give its physical and energetic body time to integrate the healing, to support the positive changes to the health and well-being of the cat.

By protecting the cat's energy, you are giving it every chance to heal for its greatest good. By protecting your energy, you are minimising the chance of giving the cat your own energy or emotions.

When working with energy, you need to understand that it overlaps, it intertwines. There are ways you can reduce the impact of this and allow the Universal energy to flow through you, rather than give the cat energy from you.

You need to ground and protect your own energy and that of the cat.

Let's cover yours first.

When?
Before you begin to work with a cat, even if working remotely or from a picture.

Why?
To ensure that you can be a working, effective healing channel and to make sure that you don't transfer any of your own energy or emotions onto the cat or take on any of the cat's energy. Energy is powerful and we need to respect it, and you.

How?
If you are pushed for time or something happens unexpectedly, you can simply take a brief moment and see yourself in a suit of armour or imagine angel wings coming down around your body or being engulfed and held in a coloured dome of light.

This is simple and really does work. Setting an intention, even in a brief second, will impact your body, spirit and energy.

If you have a little more time – and this is my preferred method – you can take a few minutes to ground and protect yourself using the Calm Connection. This is a method that I teach in all of my classes and workshops and that I use frequently myself. It is simple but highly effective and takes less than five minutes.

Calm connection:

- Sit with your back straight and feet flat on the floor, body softened, eyes closed.
- Take a steady, slow, long, deep breath.
- Then take a second and third deep breath while putting your left hand on your heart and your right hand on your solar plexus (tummy) or sacral chakra (under your belly button) – whichever feels most comfortable.
- Continue with your eyes closed to let your breath settle and find its natural rhythm. Keep breathing.
- Allow your awareness to come into the present moment by focussing on your breath, noticing it coming in and out of the body.
- Visualise roots coming out from the soles of your feet and going down through the layers of the Earth into its core. You might like to visualise a light or crystal at the core.
- On the next in-breath, draw the light up through your roots into the soles of your feet. As you breathe, keep drawing the light up through your body.
- Bring the light/energy out of the top of your head and let it fall down around your body like a protective egg shape, meeting again at your feet.

- You can visualise attaching a padlock to the energy at your feet or send the light back down into the Earth.
- Take a few moments to feel grounded, protected and held.
- Come round and open your eyes when you're ready.
- You're good to go!

The more you do the Calm Connection, or a version of it, the more you will find a style and visual format that works for you. Some people like to go into a golden egg or bubble; others will use a certain colour to put in or around their body. There is no right or wrong, but it is a crucial step in preparing yourself for a healing treatment. Let you intuition guide you as to what feels right for you.

The cat's energy

Protecting your cat is very similar to the process we have covered above. You need to ground the cat's energy using your intention and visualisation.

When I begin a healing session, I like to use the infinity symbol (a sideways figure of eight) and visualise myself in one half and the cat in the other. This helps to create a deep connection between the two of us.

Then you can visualise roots coming out from the pads of the cat's feet and going down into the Earth. You may be shown/see coloured roots. If not, use a golden or white light set of coloured roots. See them going down through the layers of the Earth and either into a crystal at the core of the Earth or simply going into a white/golden ball of light.

If you feel drawn to, you can draw the light up through the roots and into the feet of the cat – see how you are guided.

We use roots for the cat to ensure its energy and spirit are connected to the Earth, it is grounded, and its body and spirit can tolerate and process the healing energy that will move through him/her.

If we protect the cat's energy at the beginning of a session, the healing that comes through you will not be as effective. Waiting until the end of the healing session to protect the cat ensures that its aura develops no holes, thus keeping the healing energy about its body for as long as is needed.

Make sure you disconnect your energy at the end of the healing session by cutting through the middle of the figure of eight either with your hands in front of you or in your mind's eye.

Setting the scene for a chakra clearing

When you go for a massage, how do you want to feel? Relaxed, detached, peaceful, etc. It is the same for cats.

Cats are both a predator and prey animal, which means they are often on alert. They need to ensure they are not threatened before they can open up and lean into the healing. That's why some cats will come and sit with you, rub/roll and stretch out when having healing. For others, you might be working with them from behind the sofa! Every cat is unique and perfect as it is.

Let's look at what you need to consider to help your cat lean into the healing and get the most from your treatment.

Environment

You may plan to hold a session with your cat at a particular time or in a certain location. You may also find that your cat demonstrates signs of needing/wanting the healing at a time that works for him/her – but not necessarily for you!

Be open but be prepared. It's important for cats to feel safe when they are having healing. Leo usually has his healing in the evenings, when the energy in the home is calmer and, to be honest, when my energy is lighter as I prepare to go to bed.

Baby Max enjoys healing whenever he needs it. I can be sitting in the front room, and he'll pop up onto my lap. My hands start to get warm, so we have a short healing session.

If you are taking the time to plan the session, be sure to consider what's best for the cat. For instance, what is the environment like?

The more you are comfortable with your healing skills, the more you may find your cat seeks you out for a treatment when they need it.

If there are other cats or animals in the home, I recommend shutting them out of the room. If there is more than one cat in the room, your energy, focus and intention will be split.

This also goes for other human family members. It's important to be present with the cat you are working with. Remove all distractions so you can feel into the session.

Some cats may need additional reassurance to lean into the healing. You may need to provide verbal reinforcement if the cat is on high alert or simply be patient, sitting with an open posture and sending love to the cat in that moment.

What does the cat need?

Energy can be unpredictable. Therefore, I always advise that regardless of where you are working with a cat in the home, make sure it has access to fresh, untainted water, a small amount of food and a litter tray (even if 'it normally goes outside').

The litter tray may seem extreme, but if you shift a persistent blockage, the cat will need to release the energy. Don't be caught out!

Ideally, cats should be fed before the session. Don't work with a hungry cat because its behaviour can be unpredictable, and it is unlikely to be able to fully lean into the healing.

The reason I suggest having a small amount of food out is that after the healing has commenced and the energy has shifted, cats may be hungry and need fuel to enable the healing energy to assimilate fully into their bodies and auric fields.

When is the right time to heal your cat?

There is no right or wrong time to connect with and work with your cat. You will notice that the more you work with your cat and offer healing, the more it will seek you out for additional healing sessions!

You may start off by offering healing at a quiet time, perhaps just before you go to bed. Or you may like to do it at a certain time of day, perhaps before the kids come home.

Always ask your cat's permission before you try to connect with it and/or work with its energy. Cats will give you a very clear 'no thank you' by walking away.

Never force healing or energy work on your cat; its permission is crucial. If the cat doesn't want to heal, it won't.

Enjoying a session with your cat can be such a beautiful experience. It can really deepen your connection, love and bond with your cat.

Pickle enjoying a healing session on our bed – a place she felt safe, secure and comfortable.

How to sense an imbalance

The best tool you have for sensing an imbalance in a cat is your intuition. When you start to work with a cat, you may immediately notice that it directs a particular body part to you, or you notice a hot/cold spot when you stroke them. Trust what you are shown/feel/sense.

It is important to respect the cat's energy and be as systematic as possible when working with the chakras to ensure you provide a state of balance. Grounding is the first step to take to prepare you both for the session, ending with disconnecting your energy.

I mention hand positions further on, but if you can't physically touch or get near a cat, use your intention or a picture/image of the cat. It helps to take a few moments to see what you can sense or feel before you begin working with the chakras. Some cats may not tolerate touch or even be comfortable being present with a human. That's why you can use a picture, if needed.

You need to have something to focus your intention on that directs you to the cat you are working with. If the image doesn't have the full length of the cat, you can ask (either out loud or from your heart space) about the state of each chakra. The more you practise working with energy and receiving the cat, the more you will be able to feel its chakras.

Positioning your hands on or near the cat when working with the chakras if you are physically present with the cat is not a linear experience. When I work with Leo, I will frequently have a particular method/structure in mind, but he will guide me to what he needs. For example, if I position myself to start at his root, he may get up and turn around if he needs the energy work to begin at another part of his body.

Trust where your hands are guided or what your cat shows you and use your intuition to sense and shift the energy.

Here you can see a cat enjoying healing of his throat chakra. He preferred a hands-off approach.

Sensing energy

Energy will feel different for every human and every cat. For some, it will be a tingling or fizzing sensation. For others, it could feel like little bubbles or a popping sensation under the hand or fingers. You may also notice temperature changes. There is more on this in the reducing and increasing energy section further on.

Before you begin a session, start by getting an understanding of what energy can feel like in your hands. Rub your hands together, up and down or forwards and backwards. After a couple of seconds, slowly start to pull your hands apart a couple of centimetres.

Then pulse your hands to and fro and see what you sense and feel. When you rub your hands together, you create energy. As you pulse your hands to and fro you are starting to understand how energy actually *feels* for you.

When you then start to work with the cat, begin by gently stroking its aura, the space just above its physical body. To do this, run your hand down the full length of the cat, hovering just a couple of centimetres above their physical body. Take note of any temperature changes, fizzing or other sensations. Do this three times. You are sensing any initial imbalances and removing negative energy stuck in its aura.

After you have cleansed the aura, it is very typical for cats to either a) start to clean themselves – they are removing the energy you have displaced – or b) settle into a comfortable position, ready to receive the healing from you.

Starting a healing session with Leo.

In this picture, Leo had settled down after I cleansed his aura. I began his healing session with my hands near his root. As I placed my hands on him, he startled and woke up, staring at my hands. It felt like a sign from him that he didn't want hands to touch him for the healing, so I continued the session with my hands held a couple of centimetres above his physical body. If Leo hadn't wanted the healing, he would have left the area.

I started his session at the root chakra, ensuring that he was grounded and ready to receive the healing.

My hands have moved up to Leo's sacral chakra.

As my hands started to cool whilst working at his root, I felt drawn to move my hands up to his sacral chakra.

Keep your hands in place for as long as you feel drawn to. You may notice the cat slightly moves or twitches, which would indicate this chakra has been balanced and it is time to move to the next one.

And now they are working with his solar plexus.

Work through each chakra in turn if you can. The cat will show you or share with you what it needs.

I held my hands along Leo's spine for the solar plexus chakra to maintain the same distance and flow around his body. Be guided by your intuition.

As I've mentioned, the chakras are not single-entry points for energy. As long as you are working in the space of the chakra with the intention to heal it, you will be.

Ideally, you would work through each chakra in turn, sensing its energy, clearing, cleansing and balancing each one as you go. Try not to miss out a chakra.

Although it won't have a detrimental effect on the overall healing of the cat, it may make the healing session slightly less effective. This is because rather than the whole energy body being balanced and enabling the emotional, mental and physical body to simply heal, more effort will be taken by the energy to redistribute and balance throughout the cat's energetic body.

Notice how my hands are still slightly above Leo's physical body whilst he enjoys the healing around his heart.

After working with Leo's root, sacral, solar plexus and heart chakras I manoeuvred my hands to balance his throat, third eye and crown. In this instance, I couldn't position my hands directly near the crown and third eye due to Leo's sleeping position, so I held my hand around his collar and set in my heart the intention to heal each chakra in turn.

After working through all seven chakras, I thanked Leo for the opportunity to work with him and then disconnected our energetic connection, ending the session with a visualisation of protection for Leo to integrate the energy we had worked with for his highest and greatest good.

Removing stagnant energy

When we clear, cleanse and balance chakras, we are giving cats the capacity to thrive in their environment, feeling healthy, whole, balanced and grounded.

Reducing energy imbalances can help to reduce or remove 'problem behaviours' such as overgrooming, inappropriate toileting around the home or aggressive outbursts.

When a cat is balanced energetically, it helps it to feel good physically, emotionally and mentally, which leads to a balanced spirit and living in a place of joy.

Blockages of energy can be persistent and may not shift fully during one healing session. That is why making notes of what you experience during the session is crucial, as you may notice small changes over a longer period of time.

Blockages will present themselves in many ways, usually either as an incredibly hot area on the body or a noticeably cold spot when you are stroking the aura.

You may also notice a lump/bump/raised area on the cat's body. This is likely to be caused by a collection of energy, but if you have any concerns, you should always consult your vet.

Blockages can occur for a number of reasons, including physical trauma or continued stress, emotional upset, mental health decline or changes in the environment.

We don't always know what causes an energy imbalance. Sometimes it can be something we as humans may consider inconsequential, yet to our feline friends it has caused a ripple in their energy flow. We don't need to know WHY our cat has an imbalance; we just need to focus on how we can help it to shift that imbalance and find a sense of wellness again.

A cat may only be able to tolerate a small shift of energy at a time. Don't go in all guns blazing if you find a blockage; cats are VERY sensitive creatures, and you need to be guided by the cat when dealing with a blockage. Go at the cat's pace.

Also, be prepared for the cat to show distressing behaviours as you shift the energy. They may hiss, yowl or – in extreme cases – retch or vomit as they release the energy. Make sure you familiarise yourself with the 'Cat signs of energy processing' table in Part 1.

Don't be alarmed if your cat demonstrates a big energy shift; it should settle afterwards. When cats shift energy, it can seem to have extreme reactions, but as long as you are prepared for the response, you can simply hold the intention to keep the energy balanced as the cat shifts. When a blockage is shifted, there needs to be a form of release.

Reducing and increasing energy

To sense if a chakra is over- or underactive, you will need to get comfortable with 'pulsing' the chakra and feeling the energy.

In my experience, a cold chakra is underactive, and a hot chakra is overactive – but you may experience the opposite. If you need clarification, either ask your intuition, connect with and ask the cat, or use your pendulum.

To charge a chakra, move your hands/the crystal in a clockwise motion until you feel a sense of resistance or until your hand/crystal jerks and moves away.

To reduce the amount of energy in a chakra, use an anticlockwise motion. When reducing the energy in a chakra, you will generally know that you have shifted enough energy because the cat will move (stretch, twitch, yawn, etc.).

Opening, closing and protecting the chakras

Energy flows where intention goes. One of your most powerful tools when working with the chakras is your intention. As stressed earlier, it is best to work systematically through each chakra. I use a lotus flower to visually represent each chakra, but you may be more comfortable with a ball of light or another visual example. Also, the cat may show you something, so be open to receiving.

I use a lotus flower because it is easy to see in my mind's eye: opening the flower bud – opening the chakra. Charging/balancing the chakra – colours or position of the petals being even. Closing of the chakra – close the petals in towards the middle and see the flower as a bud. Surround the bud in white or golden light to protect it.

The more you work with cats, the more you will find a way that works for you. Regardless of what you 'see', you need to make sure that you open, cleanse/charge/balance and close each chakra.

When you start to work with energy, you may need to 'see' it. You can visualise a cloud-like substance as a visual for the energy. You may even see patches or a cloud/smoke-like substance in your mind's eye dark if you feel a blocked chakra.

How to conduct the session

Every session will be different. The more sessions you have, the more you will find your own rhythm and flow. To start you off, here is a guide to hosting a session with your cat:

1. **Set the scene:** As we mentioned before, remove all other animals and humans if possible. Enjoy the private connection with your cat.
2. **Preparation:** Be sure to have all essential resources in the space you are with for the cat, food, water, litter tray.
3. **Intention:** Set your intention for the session. It can be as simple as 'to help my cat heal', or something more specific, e.g. 'to reduce my cat's anxiety'. There is no right or wrong but remember that energy flows where intention goes.
4. **Comfort:** Get comfortable – regardless of whether you are physically touching the cat for the session or working at a distance, make sure you are comfortable before starting the session.

5. **Grounding:** Take a deep breath or use the Calm connection to ground and centre yourself.
6. **Protection:** After you have grounded yourself be sure to protect your own energy in whichever manner feels best for you.
7. **Permission:** Ask the cat for permission to work with it and its energy, either out loud or in your head. Either way, you will receive an indication from the cat of its response.
8. **When your cat says no:** If the cat leaves or walks away, don't be disheartened. Thank it for its honesty and try again another time.
9. **Open your heart:** If the cat agrees, focus your intention on opening your heart and making a connection with the cat. Visualise a sideways figure of eight (infinity symbol): you in one part and the cat in the other.
10. **Connect:** If the cat lets you touch it physically, stroke it three times to clear its aura and make a connection. If you can't get near the cat, visualise yourself doing it. Intention is key. See yourself and the cat in that infinity symbol, connecting your spirits and enabling the cat to receive healing energy through you.
11. **Reassure:** Some cats may not initially be open to physical touch and may require verbal reassurance from you that it is safe to lean into the healing. Remember, you are not

forcing the cat to receive it; you are simply providing reassurance if needed.
12. Ground the cat: This process is always the first step in the treatment after you have made the connection with the cat. He/she needs to be connected to the Universal energies to enable it to work with the healing energy.
13. Navigation: Use your hands (on the cat, just above or from a distance) and, working from the root chakra towards the crown, feel into each chakra in turn.
14. Follow the six steps: Open, cleanse, balance, charge, close and protect each chakra in turn.
15. Visualisation: If you feel drawn to keep your hands in the same place, use visualisation to cleanse, charge and protect each chakra point on the cat.
16. Hands on or hands off: You may use a mixture of hands on or hands above the cat during one session.
17. Closing: To close the session, visualise roots coming out from the cat's feet and going down into the ground to ground its energy, being and spirit.
18. Protect: You also need to protect the cat's energetic field, so visualise its whole body in a golden or white bubble of light.
19. Disconnect: Finally, visualise yourself and the cat in the infinity symbol and cut it through

the middle to disconnect your energetic connection and end the session.
20. **Balance residual energy:** Before you leave the cat, gently stroke the cat physically or just above its body, to balance any residual energy.
21. **Quite time:** Ensure there is quiet time at the end of the session to allow the cat to integrate and process the healing. Don't let children or other animals in the room straight away.

How to conduct a session (short version)

If you cannot be present with a cat to conduct a session with it in person, you are short of time or doing a session remotely, you can use the short chakra clearing and charging method to balance and align the cat's energy. You may want to use a toy or an image of the cat to focus your energy and intention.

It is important that you ground and protect yourself, even for a remote session. Energy is powerful; we need to respect it. You can work through each chakra in turn or use a pendulum to notice energy imbalances.

Key points to note during this type of session:

- Ground and protect yourself before and after a session.
- Ask for permission to connect with the cat.
- Work through the energy centres in turn.
- Close and protect each chakra – even if you only directly work with/cleanse/balance one specific chakra.
- Ground and protect the cat.
- Disconnect your energy.

Aftercare advice

When a chakra session is over, it is important to give the cat time and space to integrate and process the healing. This will look different for each cat and will also vary after each session.

Common responses from the cat include:

- Sleeping
- Changes in appetite
- More/less physically affectionate
- Increased cleaning activity as they continue to shift the energy
- Withdrawal from the family
- Hiding in unusual places
- Excess energy – running around the house being more playful.

All of these listed responses should reduce or return to normal within 24 hours of the treatment.
Any prolonged changes to your cat's version of 'normal' should be investigated and checked by your vet, if appropriate.

Give your cat space and time. Working with the Universal healing energy can be intense, so it is best to give your cat the respect and privacy it may need to integrate the healing.

Energy changes can affect the physical, mental, emotional and spiritual bodies of the cat. Sometimes it may only affect one layer; other times it will be more.

As we know, cats will do what they please and at their own pace, so be sure to support your cat in its healing integration in any way you can. That may include leaving him/her alone for as long as it needs.

If your cat is on any medication, be observant of their behaviours and patterns after a healing treatment. Remember my experience with Pickle on the sofa? After we shared that time together and I used the mantra of 'Help me heal her', her blood glucose level was the lowest I had ever seen!

Energy is powerful and it can help to boost the body's natural immune response. Energy has the capacity to help the systems of the body to re-align and revive from illness or incapacity.

Final words

'You did it, Mum. You opened their hearts; you helped them to see their wisdom. The light inside every one of them will grow.
As they awaken to their power, their capacity for healing and loving their cats will rise. Their inner light will shine. As they step into their strength, they believe in their truth, and they honour their cat, the two will become one. You have spoken for the cats and given them their voice.'
- Pickle.

I had no idea when I sat with Pickle on the sofa that our experience would lead me to helping you and your cat through this book. I hope that as you have implemented the tools and techniques we have covered, you feel proud of how far you have come.

Being able to support our cats energetically and emotionally is a real gift and truly empowers us as their guardians.

As this book shows, the connection we can share with our cats is undeniably profound. The journey into the mystical world of cat chakras has reinforced the importance of nurturing that bond, providing love, care and a holistic approach to their well-being.

It is my intention that you understand that cat chakra healing is an ongoing journey of discovery and growth. It is a path of elevating your understanding of your cat companion, cultivating your intuition and embracing the power of energy healing.

Regular energy work with your cat will help it to achieve a sense of health and well-being, whilst strengthening your relationship and deepening your connection with him/her. With every step you take, be sure to witness the remarkable resilience and capacity for healing that cats possess.

With daily, weekly or even monthly chakra cleanses and energy balancing sessions, you can support your cat using a holistic approach that not only will work in tandem with traditional Western medicine but will in fact boost your cat's natural healing mechanism in its own body.

I hope this book serves as a guide and inspiration for all who embark on the path of cat chakra healing, encouraging you to listen more closely to the subtle language of energy.

Allow your feline friend, with its unique essence and wisdom, to illuminate your life and remind you of the intense connections that exist between all beings.

Enjoy your next steps as you now feel equipped to begin an extraordinary journey of cat chakra healing, knowing that we all hold the ability to facilitate healing, growth and a sense of well-being for our cherished feline companions.

Be inspired to explore how your own energy and emotional state can influence your cat and vice versa.

This book has hopefully emphasised the importance of maintaining a positive and harmonious energetic environment. By incorporating meditation and self-care practices, you can foster a balanced and healing presence for you and your cat.

Enjoy, explore and tap into the energy that is all around you.

I believe you can do it. Now you have to believe in yourself. Happy healing!

If you'd like additional support about energy work with your cat or connecting with them on a soul level, visit my website and see how I can support you both.

www.naturallycats.co.uk

Appendices

Recommended reading

Here is a list of recommended reading to support your knowledge, understanding and personal growth and development:

- The Aromatic Cat – Nayana Morag & Julie-Anne Thorne
- How to Heal your Life – Louise Hay
- The Energy Codes – Dr Sue Morter
- Animal Soul Contracts – Tammy Billups
- Crystal Healing for animals – Martin J. Scott & Geal Mariani
- Heart to Heart – Pea Horsley
- Put your intuition to work – Lynn A Robinson

- How to Heal Your Pet – Elizabeth Whiter
- Cat Massage – Maryjean Ballner
- Animal Self-Medication – Caroline Ingraham
- Acu-Cat – Nancy Zidonis

Mantras for healing

- I fill this XX (cat/chakra/body) with divine light. May it sparkle and shine from within.
- All you need is inside you.
- You are a divine expression of light; you are free to shine.
- You are safe, you are held, you can be free.
- In this moment you can heal.
- I send you healing, take what you need.
- May this light heal you and the energy lift your being.
- I offer you this light/energy for your greatest good.
- Heal as you need to.
- I hold this space for you to shine.
- I feel your being and see your light.
- I see you.
- I offer you peace and love in this moment. Take what you need.
- I love you.

Cat chakra quick reference guides

Chakra	Location	Colour	Mantra
Root	At the base of the tail	Red	You are safe & secure.
Sacral	Above the hips	Orange	You can feel joy and allow peace to flow through you.
Solar plexus	Centre of the back, middle of the tummy	Yellow	You are powerful and strong.
Heart	In the middle, front of the chest.	Green	You are loved, held and supported.
Throat	At the throat	Blue	You can use your voice.

Chakra	Location	Colour	Mantra
Third eye	In between their eyes	Indigo	You can trust yourself and be exactly who you are.
Crown	Just above the top of their head between the ears	Violet/white	You are a being of pure love, light and joy.

Chakra	Gland	Emotion	Element
Root	Adrenal cortex	Fear/Trust	Earth
Sacral	Ovaries/ testes	Control/ autonomy	Water
Solar plexus	Pancreas	Power	Fire
Heart	Thymus	Love	Air
Throat	Thyroid	Truth	The Ethers
Third eye	Pituitary	Connection	The Universe
Crown	Pineal	Joy	The Cosmos

Chakra	Essential oil	Dried herb
Root	Sandalwood, frankincense, ginger, vetiver, pink lotus, angelica root, jasmine, geranium	Valerian root, angelica root, ginger root
Sacral	Neroli, ylang ylang, cinnamon, rosemary, orange, mandarin, melissa	Violet leaf, catnip leaf, calendula flowers
Solar plexus	Chamomile, bergamot, frankincense, geranium, ginger, lemongrass	Calendula flowers, chamomile flowers, yarrow flowers

Chakra	Essential oil	Dried herb
Heart	Rose, lavender, angelica root, geranium	Rosebuds, jasmine flowers, angelica root, lemon balm leaf
Throat	German chamomile, nettle (powder), peppermint, spearmint	Chickweed leaf, ginger root, peppermint leaf, marshmallow root
Third eye	Bay laurel, clary sage, marjoram, vetiver, violet leaf, yarrow	Yarrow flowers, lemongrass leaf, St John's wort, linden blossom
Crown	Jasmine, rose, geranium, sandalwood, frankincense, spikenard	Hops flowers, rose buss, valerian root, lemon balm leaf

Chakra	Crystal	Frequency (THz)
Root	Garnet, smoky quartz, red jasper, bloodstone, ruby, black obsidian	400–480
Sacral	Agate, tiger's eye, carnelian, garnet, orange jasper, calcite	480–510
Solar plexus	Amber, yellow topaz, citrine, yellow calcite, sulphur, fire opal, yellow sapphire	510–530

Chakra	Crystal	Frequency (THz)
Heart	Rose quartz, jade, peridot, malachite, green tourmaline, green calcite	530–580
Throat	Turquoise, sapphire, lapis lazuli, blue topaz, angelite, blue calcite	580–675
Third eye	Purple fluorite, blue sapphire, sodalite, blue lace agate	675–700
Crown	Amethyst, selenite, diamond, white calcite, opal, moonstone	700–790

Chakras and common conditions

Concern	Chakra
Abandonment	Heart, root
Aggression	Root, heart, throat
Allergies	Sacral, third eye
Anger	Root, heart
Anxiety	Root, heart, crown
Appetite issues	Solar plexus, sacral
Asthma	Sacral, heart
Attacking	Hear, root
Bladder problems	Root, sacral
Boredom	Sacral
Brain problems	Third eye
Chewing	Throat
Circulatory issues	Sacral
Confused	Crown
Constipation	Sacral, solar plexus
Dandruff	Root
Defensive	Root, heart
Depression	All
Detached	Root and sacral
Diabetes	Solar plexus
Diarrhoea	Sacral and root
Digestion issues	Solar plexus, sacral and root
Ear discharge	Third eye, throat
Excessive vocalisation	Throat
Eye discharge	Third eye

Fear	Root, heart
Food obsessed	Solar plexus
Forgetfulness	Crown
Frustration	Heart, root
Grief	Heart
Heart problems	Heart
Hiding away	Heart, sacral and root
Hyperactivity	Crown and root
Hyperesthesia	Heart and root
Immune disorders	Heart, solar plexus, root
Insecure	Root, heart
Irritability	Crown, root
Irritable bowel syndrome	Solar plexus, sacral
Issues with urination	Sacral, root
Jealousy	Heart, third eye
Lack of motivation	Heart, sacral
Lack of play	Heart, sacral, root
Lethargy	Crown, root
Mental illness	Crown
Nausea	Throat, solar plexus
Neck issues	Throat
Nervous system issues	Solar plexus
New home	Heart, root
Old age	Crown, heart
Overeating	Throat, solar plexus
Overgrooming	Sacral, root
Pacing	Heart, solar plexus

Poor coat	Heart, solar plexus
Reluctance for touch	Heart
Reproductive issues	Sacral
Respiratory issues	Heart, solar plexus
Restless	Crown, root
Shut down	Heart, sacral, root
Sleep issues	Third eye, crown
Throat problems	Throat
Timid	Root, sacral, heart
Ulcers	Solar plexus
Unable to settle	Root, crown
Withdrawn	Root, heart, sacral

Index

A
Abandoned 102
Abuse 24, 68, 102, 114, 119, 134
Aggression 101, 103, 119, 180
Allergies 107, 129, 133, 180
Anger 103, 119, 124, 180
Anxiety 16, 66, 82, 101, 161, 180
Appetite 89, 101, 112, 118, 123, 129, 133, 166, 180
Asthma 107, 180
Aura 20, 21, 27, 31 – 36, 41, 45, 46, 88, 144, 151, 152, 157, 162
Auric field 21, 27, 31 - 33, 36, 46, 85, 147

B
Balancing 29, 35, 46, 49, 58, 65, 71, 77, 86, 99, 103, 104, 109, 115, 120, 125, 126, 131, 135, 155, 160, 169
Blockages 15, 20, 23, 24, 112, 157

C
Coat 30, 112, 118, 119, 182
Confidence 107, 111, 114
Crown chakra 36, 50, 128, 132, 134, 135, 156, 163, 180 - 182
Crystals 35, 51, 53, 60 – 64, 98, 104, 110, 116, 120, 127, 131, 135

D
Depressed 101, 130, 180
Diarrhoea 90, 180
Discharge 129, 180

E
Ears 13, 50, 130, 133, 174
Elimination 101
Energy processing 86 – 88, 91, 158
Energy release 88, 90
Energy shifting 87
Eyes 8, 13, 32, 50, 88, 89, 129, 130, 131, 141, 142, 174

F
Fatigue 101
Fear 56, 101, 103, 175, 181
Food 8, 16, 42, 57, 64, 78 – 80, 104, 113, 118, 123, 146, 147, 161, 181
Fur 12, 78, 88, 103

G
Grounding 93, 131, 137, 138, 149, 162
Gums 123, 129

H
Heart chakra 36, 50, 82, 117 – 120, 156

I
Imbalance 15, 16, 26, 36, 48, 49, 79, 98, 102, 107, 113, 119, 123, 130, 132, 134, 148, 152, 156 – 158, 165
Infection 119, 133

J
Joints 58, 83, 84

K
Kitten 12, 55, 107

L
Lethargy 101, 181

M
Mantra 17, 35, 73, 74, 103, 108, 115, 120, 125, 126, 131, 134, 167, 172
Massage 35, 57, 83 - 85, 144, 171
Medication 13, 26 - 29, 33, 56, 167, 171
Meditation 35, 73, 82, 83, 126, 131, 137, 170
Mirroring 52, 81

N
Nature 18, 33 – 35, 57, 104, 132, 138

O
Overactive 49, 77, 107, 110, 159
Overgrooming 101, 103, 107, 109, 156, 181

P
Pacing 113, 119, 181
Play 63, 104, 105, 107, 112, 113, 115, 118, 120, 133, 135, 166, 181
Protecting 93, 137, 139, 143, 160

R
Remedies 51, 64, 65, 98
Restless 107, 113, 119, 182
Root chakra 36, 50, 71, 77, 101 - 104, 109, 150, 152, 153, 156, 163, 180

S
Sacral chakra 36, 50, 53, 105 – 107, 109, 110, 141, 153, 156, 180
Sadness 40, 119
Scared 12
Scratching 20, 34, 124
Skin 102, 129, 133, 134
Sleep 13, 55, 70 – 73, 89, 107, 112, 119, 129, 130, 133, 156, 166, 182
Solar plexus chakra 36, 50, 109, 111 – 115, 126, 128, 141, 154, 156, 180
Soul contract 54, 55, 128, 171,
Stress 16, 33, 48, 59, 83, 157, 160

T
Teeth 52, 123, 129
Territory 48, 101 – 104, 107, 108, 110, 124
Third eye chakra 36, 50, 128 – 131, 156, 180
Throat chakra 36, 50, 77, 121 - 124, 126, 150, 156, 180
Trauma 24, 47, 48, 68, 91, 104, 111, 119, 157

U
Underactive 49, 77, 159
Urinary 53, 107

V
Vibrational scale 21, 22
Vocalisation 107, 124, 126, 180
Vomiting 30, 49, 90, 113, 123

W
Withdrawn 89, 101, 113, 125, 129, 182

About Julie-Anne Thorne

Julie-Anne Thorne is a cat mum, holistic cat therapist, soul activator for cat guardians, empath and author.

After completing her Psychology degree, she became guardian to Pickle, who turned out to be a very poorly cat. In the attempt to try and help Pickle to be well, Julie-Anne trained in a variety of healing modalities such as feline zoopharmacognosy, chakra and auric healing, animal healing and animal communication.

The journey with Pickle inspired Julie-Anne to create Naturally Cats, the goal of which is to provide holistic help to cats and their guardians. Using a combination of chakra sensing, cat communication, environment enrichment, healing, soul connection, behaviour modification and botanical remedies, Julie-Anne supports cats emotionally and energetically.

Julie-Anne is currently being guided by her cats Leo and Baby Max. Both boys having their own missions to help her soul to grow and evolve.

Leo with his asthma provides regular opportunities for Julie-Anne to lean into surrender to support his physical and spiritual health. Having previously been a feral cat as part of a colony Leo can appear very withdrawn or scared of human interaction. Yet the relationship that Julie-Anne has managed to create with Leo leads him to give her cuddles most mornings!

Baby Max brings Julie-Anne joy. From the upside tummy cuddles, to the remnants of a mouse left on the hallway mat! There is never a day without smiles when Baby Max is around. Coming to live with Julie-Anne as she faced a very traumatic time in her personal life Baby Max is the ray of sunshine that helps to light her way.

Julie-Anne helps to educate and support feline guardians through a mixture of online classes, webinars, workshops and her signature programme – Become a soul led cat guardian.

Her goal is to help one million cat guardians reconnect and understand their cat so they can provide for their beloved feline friend and watch them thrive rather than simply survive.

Her mission is #givingcatsavoice

Milton Keynes UK
Ingram Content Group UK Ltd.
UKHW020106280923
429404UK00011B/58